He

Larry W...

THE OFFICIAL
VIRGIN'S/SEX MANIAC'S JOKE BOOK.
Now he'll have you roaring with

MORE THE OFFICIAL
SEX MANIAC'S JOKE BOOK

"Do you know how to keep a sex maniac in suspense?"

"No."

"Read *More* THE OFFICIAL SEX MANIAC'S JOKE BOOK and find out."

With more than 5 million books sold, world-famous jokester Larry Wilde has kept us laughing about everyone and everything: Jews, Italians, Poles, Blacks, and Irish. Virgins. Democrats. Republicans. Golfers. Kids . . .
And any combination of the above.

MORE THE OFFICIAL
SEX MANIAC'S JOKE BOOK
does it again!

MORE
THE
OFFICIAL
SEX MANIAC'S
JOKE BOOK

LARRY WILDE

Illustrations by Ron Wing

BANTAM BOOKS
TORONTO • NEW YORK • LONDON • SYDNEY

For Robin Fields –
The super socialite-secretary
and borderline sex maniac.

MORE THE OFFICIAL SEX MANIAC'S
JOKE BOOK
A BANTAM BOOK 0 553 23900 7

First publication in Great Britain

PRINTING HISTORY
Bantam edition published 1987

Illustrations by Ron Wing

Bantam Books are published by Transworld Publishers
Ltd., 61–63 Uxbridge Road, Ealing, London W5 5SA, in
Australia by Transworld Publishers (Aust.) Pty. Ltd.,
15–23 Helles Avenue, Moorebank, NSW 2170, and in New
Zealand by Transworld Publishers (N.Z.) Ltd., Cnr. Moselle
and Waipareira Avenues, Henderson, Auckland.

Printed and bound in Great Britain by
Cox & Wyman Ltd., Reading, Berks.

NYMPHOMANIAC
*Any woman with a sex drive
greater than yours*

CONTENTS

Lewd Levity

"Did you hear about the club for nymphomaniacs?"

"No."

"The meetings are great. All you do is examine prospective members."

* * *

Stash met Betsy, a very pretty blonde, at a community dance.

Later, parked in his car, she seemed wildly in love with him. Stash immediately suggested that she marry him.

"Poor baby," she said, "don't you realize that I'm a *nymphomaniac*?"

"Honeysuckle," he replied, "I don't care if you steal, as long as you be faithful to me."

Did you hear about the nymphomanic who lost her mind at a wiener roast?

* * *

There was a young lady named Clair,
Who possessed a magnificent pair,
   Or that's what I thought
   Till I saw one get caught
On a thorn and begin losing air.

* * *

"It's really none of my business," whispered Mrs. Maloney, "but have you noticed what your daughter is doing?"

"Why, no," answered Mrs. Malavasi. "What's she up to?"

"She's knitting tiny garments," said the Irish woman.

"Well, thank goodness," said the Italian lady. "I'm glad to see she's taken an interest in something besides running around with boys."

* * *

SIGN NEAR REAL ESTATE DEVELOPMENT

Get Lots While You're Young

* * *

"Do you know how to keep a sex maniac in suspense for twenty-four hours?"

"No."

"I'll tell you tomorrow."

2

Quinn received the first letter from his soldier son.

"Dear Dad, I can't tell you where I am, but yesterday I shot a polar bear. . . ."

Several months later came another letter: "Dear Dad, I still can't tell you where I am, but yesterday I danced with a native girl. . . ."

Two weeks later, this note arrived: "Dear Dad, I still can't tell you where I am, but yesterday the doctor told me I should've danced with the polar bear and shot the native girl. . . ."

* * *

WET DREAM

A snorgasm

* * *

A sensationally stacked redhead entered a doctor's office on her lunch hour and approached a handsome young man in a white coat.

"I've had a pain in my shoulder for a week. Could you help me?" she asked.

"Lie down on this table," he said, "and I'll massage it for you."

After a few minutes the pretty gal exclaimed, "Doctor, that isn't my shoulder!"

"No," said the fellow, "and I'm not the doctor, either."

* * *

The airliner was about to crash. An American grabbed the last parachute and started buckling it on. "I say, old chap," said an Englishman, "what about the ladies?"

"Screw 'em!" exclaimed the American.

"Do you think we have time?"

* * *

Where do Manhattan virgins save for a rainy day?

The *Chaste National Bank*.

* * *

OVERHEARD AT A COCKTAIL PARTY

Alexandria: I'm hungry for a man!
Casper Milquetoast: (Meekly) I'm a man!
Alexandria: Look, I said I'm hungry, not starved!

* * *

Did you hear about the whimsical masturbator who had an offbeat sense of humor?

* * *

In the morning was beautiful Dolly
Bemoaning her nocturnal folly.
    He had looked like a funny old bloke,
    And she thought he was just an odd joke,
But the joke was on Dolly, by golly!

What did the egg say to the water?

If you'll get hot, I'll get hard, and we can both get out of here in three minutes.

* * *

Falk, 82, and Palmer, 86, had been friends for sixty years. Neither man had married, and each month they met in Central Park to talk about their sexual conquests.

One day Palmer showed up pushing a baby carriage, with a lovely teenage girl hanging on his arm and a good-looking young jock walking behind them. "Say," asked Falk, "whose baby is that?"

"Mine," answered Palmer.

"And is the girl your daughter?" asked Falk.

"Don't be a dummy. She's my wife."

"Then I suppose the fellow bringing up the rear is your father-in-law?"

"No," said the old man, "he's our go-between."

* * *

LABIA MAJORA

The curly gates

* * *

"Do you know the difference between sex and peanut butter?"

"No."

"Then you'd better stick to peanut butter!"

Bernie Sandler, the retired talent rep, related this rib-tickler:

Hazel had just finished her shower when the doorbell rang. She tiptoed to the front door, completely nude, and called, "Who is it?"

"The blind man," said the voice. Hazel opened the door with one hand while reaching for her purse with the other. When she turned to face the man, he was grinning from ear to ear, and Hazel saw that he was holding a large package in his arms.

"You can see!" she exclaimed.

"Yeah," he replied. "Where do you want me to put these blinds?"

A REAL KIBITZER

*The unmarried half of the
Siamese Twins*

* * *

O'Connor, 86, saw a little girl sitting on a front porch. She was crying. "What's the matter?" he asked.

"I want one of those things like my brother's got, that sticks out and lays down and sticks out again."

So O'Connor sat down and cried too.

* * *

Why is masturbation better than intercourse?
(1) Because you know who you are dealing with.
(2) Because you know when you've had enough.
(3) Because you don't have to be polite afterward.

* * *

There was a young girl from Knizes
With breasts of two different sizes.
    One was so small,
    It was nothing at all,
But the other was large and won prizes.

* * *

Norine went to the drugstore counter and was about to tell the clerk what she wanted. "Wait," he exclaimed, "I'm a mindreader. Let me guess what you want."

He handed her a box of Kotex, but she refused it. "You're wrong. I want some toilet paper!"

"Well," he explained, "I only missed it by that much!"

*　*　*

"Did you ever smell moth balls?"
"Sure."
"How'd you get your nose between their little legs?"

*　*　*

PORNO PREMIER REVIEW

The performance by the star of the new hard-core film was stirring. When the movie was over, there wasn't a dry fly in the house.

*　*　*

"Will you, for God's sake, stop poking that thing into me!" hissed Harriet to the man behind her in the rush-hour subway train.

"But it's only my pay envelope," countered the fellow.

"You must have some job, then. That was your third raise since we left Times Square!"

Tommy Moore, the Philadelphia comedian/ newspaper columnist, came up with this corker:

Horace was an awfully short man. One evening he was caught in the Manhattan subway crush and became jammed between the breasts of a tall, tantalizing blonde. He winked, wiggled his eyebrows, and flirted outrageously with her. Finally, the woman could bear it no longer. "Listen fresh guy," she sneered, "how would you like a bust in the mouth?"

"All right, you mind reader, you!"

Did you hear about the 55-year-old bachelor who woke up one morning feeling like a 21-year-old?

Unfortunately, he couldn't find one that early in the day.

* * *

Crawford and Mason, two elderly cronies, were having lunch in a New York restaurant.

"Listen," said Crawford, "it seems to me that there's not as much sex going on as there was back in the old days."

"Yes, there is," replied Mason. "There's just another crowd doing it."

* * *

Tany Berman, the lovable Louisville dress manufacturer, says: "Tight clothes do not stop a girl's circulation. The tighter the clothes, the more she circulates."

* * *

MacVoy, age 76, sat on a crowded bus. He said to the pretty girl standing in front of him. "Miss, you might as well sit on my lap. I'm too old to get up and give you my seat, and too old for it to be wrong to offer my lap."

The girl smiled and accepted the invitation. After jolting along in the bus for a few blocks with her bouncing on his lap, MacVoy said, "Miss, one of us will have to get up. I'm not as old as I thought I was."

Did you hear about the beautiful woman with lustrous black tresses who does 100 strokes a night?

After that, if she has any energy left, she brushes her hair.

* * *

FELLATIO

The French Connection

* * *

I don't mind if a girl rides a helicopter,
I don't mind if a girl rides a car,
    But the girl who rides straddle
    When she should ride sidesaddle
Is stretching things a bit far.

* * *

Carol and Barbi were talking about women who find older men attractive.

"Why," said Carol, "my grandfather was a real ladies' man. Women were crazy about him."

"How did your grandfather feel about it?" asked Barbi. "Was he crazy about them, too?"

"Well, not at first, but after a while it went to his head and he began to cut notches on his cane, one for every conquest. And do you know that's what killed him."

"How do you mean, that's what killed him?"

"Well, he made the mistake of leaning on his cane one day!"

Rae Alvarado, Sea Ranch's irresistible Rams Head Realtor, relayed this warm-hearted knee-slapping ribber:

Mackey and Devlin, two elderly men, were sitting on a park bench discussing their sexual situation.

"I just heard," said Mackey, "that eating oysters puts lead in your pencil. Why don't we try it?"

"I don't know about you," replied Devlin, "but at my age I don't have many women to write to."

Rudy Vallee, America's all-time air-waves crooning great, gets gaffaws with this gut-tickler:

I was down in Palm Springs at Charlie Farrell's Racquet Club, and one afternoon I noticed this elderly man sitting on the edge of the pool. It was a terribly hot day, so I said to him, "Why don't you take a dip in the water!"

"Can't," said the old man. "I've been barred from using the pool."

"Why?"

"I felt like I had to do it, so I did it in the pool."

"Nearly everyone has done it in the pool at one time or another."

"From the diving board?" he replied.

* * *

Did you hear about the two nudists who decided to stop dating because they felt they were seeing too much of each other?

* * *

An astronomer's comment was heinous:
"We should not let convention restrain us.
    Though I've made a career
    Out of Venus, my dear,
I am tempted to switch to Uranus."

* * *

Pretty Steno: Can you tattoo a cat on my knee?
Tattoo Artist: We're having a sale this week on giraffes.

Owen and Garrett went into the men's room. Owen walked up to the urinal and began to urinate. Garrett sat down in the next stall to pass water.

"Hey," asked Owen, "how come you always sit down when you're just taking a leak?"

"The doctor told me not to lift anything heavy!" replied Garrett.

* * *

Modeling can be a very rewarding career.

A good model can make $100 an hour, and a bad one can make much more.

* * *

A hockey star was being interviewed by a sports columnist. "Did you ever have a real embarrassing experience?" the reporter asked.

"Yeah," said the skater, "when my Mom caught me playing with myself."

"Oh, we all did that when we were kids."

"Yeah, but this happened yesterday."

* * *

17

Christopher had been stranded on a deserted island for many years. His clothes were in tatters, and he had a long beard. One day he suddenly began shouting, "A ship! A ship! It's heading this way. And I bet," he went on, talking to himself, "there's a gorgeous blonde on board . . . with big bouncing boobs . . . and beautifully curved hips . . . and a round, smooth ass! I can just taste her hot lips as our naked bodies come together! I can. . . ."

By then, Christopher had a large, throbbing erection. He grabbed himself and began to masturbate furiously.

"I gotcha now, you bastard," he said, laughing maniacally. "There ain't no goddamned ship!"

* * *

Free Spirit Femmes

"Darling," he whispered, "am I the first man to make love to you?"

"Of course you are," she snapped. "I don't know why you men always ask the same silly question!"

* * *

Francine, a super built bikini-clad blonde, bounced along the Santa Monica Beach.

"Hey, there," called a horny Hollywood type, "you're the best thing I've seen all day! Why don't you stop, so I can look a little longer?"

"No need to," said Francine. "You're beginning to look a little longer already."

She wasn't what one would call pretty,
And other girls offered her pity;
    So nobody guessed
    That her Wasserman test
Involved half the men of the city.

* * *

Julie was quite calm when the doctor told her the news.

"Don't you have any idea who fathered your unborn child?" asked the M.D.

"Doc," said Julie, "if you backed into a buzz saw, could you tell which tooth was the sharpest?"

* * *

Jack: Do you believe in free love?
Jane: Have I ever given you a bill?

* * *

MONEY MEDLEY

She was only the paymaster's daughter, but she made advances to all the men.

* * *

"I'm very sorry, Paul," she said. "I can never learn to love you."

"Gee, that's too bad," said Paul, "and after I'd saved fifty grand, too."

"Give me one more lesson."

20

INTELLECTUAL WOMEN'S LIBBER

*One who can think up excuses that her
boyfriend's wife will believe.*

* * *

The world-famous feminist was giving a
speech in support of the Equal Rights Amendment. Suddenly she was interrupted by the deep
voice of a heckler from the crowd: "Don't you
wish you were a man?"

"No," she replied. "How about you?"

* * *

Lou: Do you like codfish balls?
Sue: I don't know . . . I've never balled one.

* * *

"How did you enjoy Rome?"

"There's so much fanny-pinching there,
I'd classify the city as an ass-felt jungle."

* * *

Kitty Steele, the beautiful Beverly Hills
exec sec, evokes belly laughs with this bauble:

During the floods in southern California, a
first-aid worker stuck his head into a school
gym being used as a shelter for the homeless
victims and asked, "Are there any pregnant
women in here?"

"For crying out loud," shouted a woman,
"we're not even dry yet."

Zetta Castle, La Costa's public relations queen, contributed this little cutie:

The new tenant was fumbling with the lock to the door of his apartment. Suddenly, he turned around and saw Doreen, a luscious blonde with her arms full of packages. "Hi, there!" she greeted him. "I'm the Welcome Lady with a few settling-in presents for you and your wife."

"Thanks," said the man, "but I'm not married."

Doreen dropped the packages on the floor and said, "In that case, we won't need this junk, will we?"

FELLATIO PHILOSOPHY

*Girls who don't repulse men's
advances—advance men's pulses.*

* * *

Helen and Agnes, two swingers from the steno pool, were on their coffee break.

"How was your blind date last night?" asked Helen.

"He turned out to be your ex-boyfriend," replied Agnes, "and, believe me, now I know why you referred to him as the wild Texas longhorn."

* * *

At one of the wildest parties he'd ever been to, Creighton noticed a very prim and pretty girl sitting quietly apart from the rest of the revelers. Approaching her, he introduced himself and said, "I'm afraid you and I don't really fit in with this jaded group. Why don't I take you home?"

"All right," said the girl, "Where do you live?"

* * *

There was a young girl of Dumfries,
Who said to her boyfriend, "Oh, please,
    It will give me great bliss
    If you play more with *this*,
And give less attention to *these*!"

* * *

Motto seen on the wall of a women's executive club: FAINT HEART NEVER WON FUR, LADY.

* * *

A foolish young woman named Alice
Used a dynamite stick for a phallus.
    They found her vagina
    In North Carolina
And the rest of poor Alice in Dallas.

* * *

Melinda Corey, the chic Chicago literary rep, loves this ribald reveler:

Sloan and Joyce had been out to dinner, listened to some jazz, and were standing outside her apartment door. "I'm sorry, but you can't come in," she said. "My roommate's home."

"In other words," said Sloan, "I'm supposed to ignore this doormat that says, 'Welcome'?"

"Of course, silly," she laughed. "There certainly isn't room enough for us on that!"

* * *

A kinky night-coach passenger boarded the plane and, with a big grin, exposed himself to the stewardess.

"I'm sorry," said the girl, "but you'll have to show me your ticket, not your stub."

* * *

Vinnie Wanderman, New York's hat check concession Czar, came up with this crackerjack:

Penny, a pretty young redhead, got a job as a driver with a cross-country bus company. On her first run from Kansas City to Phoenix the big bus broke down on the prairie, and there was no tool kit aboard.

Penny had her head in the engine when a handsome State Trooper drove up and asked facetiously, "How about a screwdriver?"

"Why not," said Penny, "it'll help pass the time until the repair crew gets here."

27

Frankie managed to get a date with Adrian, the company sexpot. To impress her with his athletic ability, Frankie took her out iceskating. Adrian was not the outdoor type, so while Frankie twirled gaily on the blades, she stayed in the lodge. After an hour out in the cold, Frankie came in to warm up. He whipped off his mittens and put his hands under Adrian's skirt. "Hey, what do you think you're doing?" she yelled as she felt his hands press between her thighs.

"Well, it's so cold out there, I just thought I'd warm my hands a little bit," he replied.

Then off he went out into the cold. Twenty minutes later he returned to the lodge and again placed his hands between Adrian's thighs.

This went on several times, and finally as he made another appearance at the lodge door, Adrian snapped, "Say, don't your ears ever get cold?"

* * *

FREE SPIRIT FEMME PHILOSOPHY

A girl must use what Mother Nature gave her before Father Time takes it away.

* * *

There was a young woman named Dee,
Who slept with each man she did see.
   If it came to a test,
   She wished to be best—
And practice makes perfect, you see.

* * *

M—is for the many times you laid me:
O—is for the other times you tried.
T—is for the trailer camp we stayed in;
H—is for the hell we raised inside.
E—is for the everlasting pleasure,
R—is for the rubbers we forgot.
   Put them all together, they spell
   MOTHER. And baby, that's what I'm
   gonna be!

* * *

Janice returned from a heavy date with her new boyfriend. "Mother," she said, "tonight Rodney popped the question."

"You mean he finally asked you to marry him?"

"No, he wanted to know whether I wanted to do it in a motel or save money by doing it in his car."

VAGINA

The tunnel of love

* * *

Little Beth walked into a drugstore and asked the clerk, "Do you fit men for trusses here?"

"Why, yes, we do," he replied.

"Well, wash your hands," said the child. "I want a chocolate soda."

* * *

There was a young lady named Gloria,
Whose boyfriend said, "May I explore ya?"
   She replied to the chap,
   "I will draw you a map
Of where others have been to before ya."

* * *

"How come you're so upset?" asked Edie of her returning roommate.

"Of all the damn nerve," said Leila, "he just handed me a vibrator and told me to buzz off!"

* * *

Berta admitted to her mother that she was going to have a baby but didn't know who the father was. "But you must know!" insisted the mother.

"How *can* I know," shouted Berta. "There were twelve guys at the surprise party!"

* * *

Ellie and Curt got into an argument over whether it was possible for a man to rape a strong girl.

They tried and he won.

"You didn't win fair!" exclaimed Ellie. "My foot slipped. Let's try it again!"

* * *

NYMPHOMANIA

Aye trouble

One Friday morning a Manhattan fashion model arrived at her beauty shop. "Give me a casual, sexy look," she said. "I'm spending the weekend in bed with a man."

"Oh," said the hairdresser, "is it anyone you know?"

* * *

Sheila, a lusty young swinger, strolled into the health club sauna. An older lady noticed she had no pubic hair. "How come?" she asked.

"Did you ever see grass grow on a busy street?" replied Sheila.

* * *

Gladys went to an artists' ball stark naked. The doorman refused to admit her. "Nudity is okay," he said. "But you've got to represent something!"

She came back wearing black gloves and shoes.

"You're just as bad as you were before," said the doorman. "What are you supposed to be?"

"Can't you see?" said Gladys. "I'm the five of spades."

* * *

Billie: (From bedroom) Has the mail-man come yet?
Her Roommate: (From kitchen) No, but he's breathing hard!

31

Gilbert Miller, Hollywood's top talent rep, tantilizes listeners with this titillator:

Unbeknownst to him, Crandall was sitting in a restaurant with his pants unzipped. A grey-haired spinster at a nearby table nearly choked on her salad when she spotted it. Immediately, the old maid wrote a note and had it delivered to Crandall.

Unfolding the note, he read, "Young man, I'm sure you don't know it, but your fly is unzipped and you are exposing yourself. You ought to be ashamed to be in a public place and not have the decency to behave like a gentleman.

"P.S. I love you."

Herb spent a fantastic night with Sharon, the blonde he had picked up at a single's bar. In the morning he said, "Do you need any money?"

"No," she said. "I never take money from a friend. But there's a hardware store downstairs that sells Swiss army penknives with five blades. You could buy me one of those."

Herb bought her the Swiss army penknife, and when he gave it to her, she put it in a drawer filled with similar pocket knives.

"That's kind of strange," he said. "Why do you save those things?"

"Right now I'm young and pretty, and I can get all the men I want," said Sharon, "but some day I'll be old and men won't give me a tumble. You know a Boy Scout will do *anything* for a Swiss Army penknife with five blades."

* * *

TIMID FEMINIST

A chicken libber

* * *

There was a young lady from Senn,
Who said, "Let us do it again
   And again and again
   And again and again
And again and again and AGAIN!"

* * *

A befuddled Chicky named Ida
Said to Gavin as he slid it insider.
   "I'd much rather be
   Underneath as 'ridee'
Than on top in the role of the rider."

*   *   *

Margo, Charlotte, and Ella were recalling the greatest thrill of their lives.

"Mine," said Margo, "was on my wedding night."

Charlotte said, "My greatest thrill was when I first saw my first child."

Ella, still unmarried, said, "I had my greatest thrill when my cockeyed sister gave me an enema."

*   *   *

Flora was walking through the woods when suddenly a frog spoke to her. "Pretty lady, I am really a prince. A wicked witch transformed me into a frog. But she said that if a pretty girl would take me home and hold me close to her bosom, the next morning I'd be lying beside her, a tall, handsome prince with big, broad shoulders."

Flora took the frog home, held it to her bosom all night, and sure enough, next morning lying beside her was a tall, handsome prince with big, broad shoulders.

Do you know that until this day Flora's mother doesn't believe that story?

*   *   *

Amusing Animals

There was a young farmer named Morse,
Who fell madly in love with his horse.
  Said his wife, "You rapscallion,
  That horse is a stallion—
This constitutes grounds for divorce."

* * *

Mrs. Higelmire had been plucking feathers from a live rooster for a family dinner. But when her son phoned to say he couldn't come, the meal was postponed. Feeling sorry for the undressed rooster, she made him a small pair of pants.

Soon her husband came into the house, laughing hysterically.

"What's wrong?" asked the wife.

"Funniest thing I ever saw," he replied. "That rooster is holding a hen down with one foot and trying to unbutton his pants with the other."

By 1640 the Jamestown colony had settled into sinful ways. At the town meeting Captain John Smith berated the colonists for their evil conduct. "Terrible deeds are being done," he shouted. "Men are illicitly knowing their neighbors' wives and daughters; men are having vile relations with other men. And there is bestiality —human beings fornicating with dogs and cats, horses and cows, pigs, sheep, chickens. . . ."

From the back of the room came a voice: "*Chickens*?"

* * *

Have you heard about the butcher who opened a new establishment and rewarded his first twenty women customers with a free goose?

* * *

WILD GOOSE

One that is an inch off center

* * *

Stephanie Olsson, the lovely Los Angeles Bank exec, likes this loony bit of levity:

Connie the cow stood on one side of the barbed wire fence. Barnaby the bull was on the other side. Connie winked at Barnaby, and he leaped over the fence to her side.

Flirting with him, Connie batted her eyelashes and asked "Aren't you Barnaby, the bull?"

"Not anymore," he squeaked. "That fence was higher than I thought."

A bird breeder was showing off his hybrids to some visitors. "This," he said, "is a cross between a chicken and a turkey. We call it a churkey."

"This is a cross between a chicken and a goose. We call it a choose."

"And this is my masterpiece—a cross between a pheasant and a duck. We call it George."

* * *

While Marge was vacationing in the country one day, she saw a young boy coming down the road leading a huge bull.

"Where are you going with that bull?" she asked.

"To service a cow down the road," said the young farmer.

"Couldn't your father do it?"

"No, it's got to be the bull."

* * *

What's the best way to make a bull sweat?
Give him a tight jersey.

* * *

Why does a cow have a long face?
If you had your tits pulled twice a day and were screwed only once a year, you'd have a long face too.

* * *

On a small South Pacific Island the white missionary was visited by the chief of the tribe.

"What's the trouble?" asked the religious leader.

"A white baby be born in the village," replied the native. "We no like white man foolin' around with our women. Since you only white man on island, tribe want to fry you alive."

The missionary almost collapsed. Then he noticed a flock of sheep on the hillside behind the village and said to the chief, "Look out there! You see that flock of white sheep?"

"Me see," replied the chief.

"Well," said the missionary, "do you see the black sheep in the middle of the flock?"

"Yes."

"It's the only one and there's never been any other black sheep."

"Okay," said the chief, "you not tell, me not tell."

Where do you get virgin wool?
From ugly sheep.

* * *

Clem and Luke, two farm hands in deep need of a woman, decided they would diddle a sheep. Clem got into a sheep, and wooed it so vigorously the animal put its tongue out.

"Holy mackerel," exclaimed Luke, "you're coming through the front!"

"All right, stick on another sheep!"

* * *

DUCK DICK

A game warden

* * *

An attractive young maiden named Myrtle
Had quite an affair with a turtle.
    And what's more phenomenal,
    A swelling abdominal
Proved to Myrtle the turtle was fertile.

* * *

A California zoo has been showing sex films to a cow and bull to encourage them to mate.

So far it hasn't worked, but the keeper and his wife close the zoo earlier every day.

* * *

42

A city girl was chased up a tree by a bull. Ten minutes later the hired hand helped her down.

"What's the matter?" he asked. "Can't you take it?"

"Sure I can take it," she replied, "but what the hell would I do with a calf in Chicago?"

* * *

Millar, a Bostonian, went to a New England farm for a weekend. On Saturday morning he watched his host's daughter milking her cow when a farm hand hollered, "Cheese it! Here comes the bull!"

Millar jumped over a fence for safety, but the girl never budged from her stool. The bull came up abruptly, snorted once, and meekly retreated to his stall. "Weren't you p-p-petrified?" stammered the Bostonian.

"No," said the daughter, "but I reckon the bull was. This here cow's his mother-in-law."

* * *

An elderly bull and his young son were standing on a hillside looking down at a herd of attractive guernseys.

"Say, Dad," said the young bull. "Let's run down and get us a couple of them cows."

"No," said the old bull, "let's *walk* down and screw 'em all!"

Charlie Harper, the brainy Bechtal engineer, breaks up buddies with this bit of burlesque:

Vivian and Neal were invited to a neighbor's costume party. Neal wore a bull costume, and Vivian dressed up like a cow. Being late, they decided to take the short cut across a field, rather than drive.

In the middle of the pasture they found themselves face to face with a real bull.

"Oh, my God," shouted Vivian, "that bull is charging right for me. What'll we do?"

"I'm just gonna stand here and eat grass," said Neal, "but you'd better brace yourself!"

Did you hear about the new insecticide they've put out this summer called Spanish Human?

It doesn't kill the flies, but it makes them so horny you can swat them two at a time!

* * *

During the early days of Rome, Paul, a Christian, was taken to the arena, tied naked to four stakes, and left to be devoured.

The cage door opened, and an enormous lion pranced out. He approached the spreadeagled victim and sniffed him hungrily. Paul had heard that a lion would not eat a dead body so he pretended to be dead.

The lion began licking the soles of his feet, and though it tickled, he kept himself from giggling.

Then the lion began licking Paul's testicles and he was horrified to feel himself getting an erection. The lion stood drooling and then began licking Paul's penis, which now stood up perfectly straight.

The lion stopped, lifted one paw, smoothed back his mane and lisped, "Oh, you ssssweet boy!"

* * *

What have you if you've got a green ball in your left hand and a green ball in your right hand?

You have Kermit the Frog's complete attention!

Newlyweds Hanna and Jim, while touring southern Florida, stopped at a rattlesnake farm. After seeing the sights, they approached the man who handled the snakes.

"Gosh!" exclaimed the new bride. "You have a dangerous job. Don't you ever get bitten by the snakes?"

"Yes, I do," answered the handler.

"Well," said Hanna, "what do you do when you're bitten by a snake?"

"I always carry a sharp knife and as soon as I'm bitten, I make deep criss-cross marks across the fang wounds and then suck the poison from the wound."

"What would happen if you were to accidentally sit on a rattler?" asked Hanna.

"Ma'am," said the snake handler, "that'll be the day I learn who my real friends are."

* * *

A maid in the land of Aloha
Got caught in the coils of a boa.
 And as the snake squeezed,
 The maid, not displeased,
Cried, "Come on and do it Samoa."

* * *

Did you hear about the snake who gave birth to a bouncing baby boa?

* * *

Joan Sheets, the dazzling cruise ship talent co-ordinator, loves this nugget of nonsense:

Trager was strolling through Central Park when he met a penguin. The penguin took an immediate liking to Trager, and it began following him. Not knowing what to do, Trager led it to a police station.

"Mister," advised an officer, "you better take it to the zoo."

The next day one of the policemen met Trager strolling with the penguin.

"What are you still goin' around with that bird for?" he said. "I thought you were gonna take it to the zoo?"

"I did," replied Trager. "And he loved the zoo, but that was yesterday. Today we're going to the movies."

A flea named Herman was sunning himself on Miami Beach when he noticed another flea, his friend Felix, shaking with cold. "Why are you shivering?" asked Herman.

"I came down to Miami," replied the other flea, "on the moustache of a guy riding a Honda."

"Next time," suggested Herman, "just crawl up the leg of a pretty girl and get into a place that's warm."

The following year, Herman was once again taking a sunbath when he noticed Felix arrive half frozen.

"Didn't you do what I told you?"

"Yeah," said Felix the flea. "I crawled up this pretty girl's leg into a place that was nice and warm. Next thing I knew I was on the moustache of a guy riding a Honda."

* * *

Why do animals lick their genitals?
Because they can.

* * *

INSECTUAL INSTINCT

Here's to the little bounding flea.
It's hard to tell the sex, you see.
It's hard to tell the he from the she,
But *she* knows, and so does *he*.

* * *

* * *

A fair farmer's daughter near Philly
Was knocked off her feet by a billy.
  She let out a quote,
   "You horny old goat,
"You ain't kiddin' *me* . . . I'm on the pilly."

* * *

A mouse and a lion were in a bar having drinks. While they were imbibing, a beautiful female giraffe wandered in, stepped up to the bar and ordered a cocktail.

Soon the mouse was flirting with the giraffe. Ten minutes later, the mouse crawled along the bar, up the giraffe's back, on to her neck and began blowing in her ear.

The two left immediately. Several hours passed and the mouse finally returned. His fur was all ruffled, his tail curled and limp, his whiskers all out of shape. "Why do you look so beat up?" asked the lion.

"I'll tell you," said the mouse, "between the kissing and the screwing, I must've run 22 miles."

* * *

An epicure dining at Crewe
Found quite a large mouse in the stew;
  Said the waiter, "Don't shout
   And wave it about
Or the rest will be wanting one too!"

51

One lovely Sunday morning, Mrs. La Motte, a crotchety old dowager, visited the San Diego zoo. She stood staring at two adjacent cages and then asked the keeper, "Young man, what is the difference between the American porcupine and the European porcupine? They look the same to me!"

"Well," answered the attendant, "there's really no difference at all except that the prick of the European porcupine is nine inches long, while that of the American porcupine is only seven."

Highly indignant Mrs. La Motte marched over to the curator's office and demanded that the attendant be discharged for indecent remarks.

"Oh!" said the curator. "You misunderstood him. What he meant was that the quill of the European porcupine is nine inches long, while the quill of the American porcupine is only seven inches long. Actually, neither one's prick is more than two inches long."

* * *

One night a girl had an affair
With a fellow all covered with hair.
    Then she picked up his hat
    And realized that
She'd been had by Smokey the Bear.

* * *

In the middle of the night Hoffman heard howls coming from his basement and went down to discover a female cat being raped by a mouse. Fascinated, he gained the mouse's confidence with some cheese and then took him next door to his neighbor's house. The mouse repeated his amazing performance with a large female German shepherd dog.

Hoffman rushed home with the mouse and woke up his wife. She saw the mouse, screamed and ducked under the blankets. "But honey," said Hoffman, "wait till I tell you about this."

"Don't come any nearer," shrieked his spouse. "Just get that *sex maniac* out of here!"

* * *

Harry: Are you an animal lover?
Barry: Well, my wife thinks so.

* * *

Mrs. Caldwell was browsing in a pet shop and came upon an unusual feathered fowl.

"This is a goony bird," said the pet-shop owner. "Its powerful beak and claws can completely demolish anything."

"How horrible," said Mrs. Caldwell.

"The bird is well behaved and completely obedient," replied the owner. "But when he's given a command, like 'Goony Bird, the chair' or 'Goony Bird, the table,' he'll attack and destroy the thing that was named."

"Could he destroy a television set?" asked the woman.

"Yes."

"I'll buy him!" said the woman, excitedly.

When she got home, Mrs. Caldwell found her husband—as usual—in front of the television set. Her once-loving spouse had lost all interest in sex, in conversation, in everything except TV. "But things will be different from now on," she thought, opening the cage.

"What'd you buy?" asked Caldwell. "A canary, a parakeet?"

"I bought a Goony Bird," she replied, about to give the command that would destroy the boob tube.

"Goony Bird, my ass!" said her husband.

* * *

Sensual Salesmen

"Your husband travels so much. Are you sure he likes your cooking?"

"Don't be silly! My Louie is nuts about the pot roast I make. In fact, when he comes home from the road, that's the second thing he asks for!"

* * *

The son of a traveling salesman was to be married the following day.

"Pop, is there anything you want to tell me before I take the big step?"

"Well, son, I have only two pieces of advice. Make your wife understand you gotta have one night a week out with the boys." Then, winking, he added, "But don't waste it on the boys!"

SALESMAN

*A fellow with a smile on
his face, a shine on his
pants, and a lousy territory.*

* * *

Marner's territory covered Tennessee. During a terrible storm he was put up overnight by a hillbilly. There was only one bed, so to save space he and his host were to sleep alternately head to heels with the mountaineer's wife and her sister. "But no foolishness," warned the mountaineer, flourishing a big six-shooter, which he then put under his pillow and fell asleep.

The sister-in-law, who was lying next to Marner, slid her hand up his leg and began fondling him. He pointed warningly to the pistol. She whispered, " 'Taint loaded," and pulled him over onto her.

Later the wife, who had been watching, said, " 'Taint loaded," and climbed over on top of Marner.

The hillbilly slept on. In a few minutes the sister-in-law slid her hand up the salesman's leg again. " 'Taint loaded!" said Marner, pointing to his penis.

* * *

SELLING SONG

*She was only a salesman's daughter,
but she gave out plenty of samples.*

Balson, a Chicago insecticide salesman, wanted an order so badly he made the farmer a special proposition. "I'll strip completely, spray myself with my company's product and then spend the night lashed to a chair in the pasture. If I remain unbitten, you give me the order; if not, I'll pay you fifty bucks!"

The farmer accepted. When he untied the salesman the following morning, he was amazed to see Balson with no bite marks. But the fellow was in a state of near exhaustion.

After some breakfast the farmer asked, "What happened?"

"Well, the insects weren't any trouble," muttered the salesman, "but doesn't that damn calf have a mother?"

*　*　*

While selling his stationery line in Milwaukee, Andrews picked up a girl and took her to his hotel room. He poured her a glass of whiskey and as he added the soda, he looked up and said, "Say when!"

"Hey," pleaded the girl, "can't I even have my drink first?"

*　*　*

Two salesmen arrived in Atlanta during a convention and were forced to share one bed in a hotel room. During the night one of them said, "Don't answer now, but are you by any chance sucking me off?"

Pete Viviani, the super Sonoma Cheese Factory impresario, sent in this snappy smiler:

Wilkins, the southern sales manager of a large Midwest firm, was making his maiden trip through Georgia. The first day he pulled up beside a farmhouse, hopped out of his car, leaped on to the porch, and rang the doorbell. A moment later, a beautifully built blonde with deep blue eyes answered his ring.

"Oh, boy," exclaimed Wilkins, "I'll bet you're the farmer's daughter!"

"No," said the girl. "I'm his mistress."

Bostwick was driving through the back roads of Tennessee when nature called. There wasn't a gas station in sight so the salesman stopped at a farmhouse.

"What can I do for yer?" asked the farmer.

"I wonder if you'd let me use your bathroom?" asked Bostwick.

"Sure thing," answered the Tennesseean. "Just go right 'round back."

Bostwick rushed to the rear of the house and found a little building with two half moons on the door. He opened it. A man sitting there said, "Come on in, the other seat's empty."

In a few minutes, the other man got up and as he pulled up his overalls some loose change fell out of his pocket down into the hole. He didn't say anything but took a $20 bill out of his other pocket and threw it down the hole.

"What did you do that for?" asked Bostwick.

"You don't think I'm going down there for thirty-five cents, do you?"

* * *

SALESMAN'S SONATA

What I like to hear most of all
And I'm sure you will say that I'm right
Is a girl who says, "I shouldn't—
But for you I will tonight."

60

Phil Klausner, the fabulous Pacific tuna fisherman, supplied this fun-filled fable:

Feldman wrote a number of large orders in Detroit and decided to celebrate. He knocked on the door of the house where a cabdriver had told him he could be sexually accommodated. A small panel opened, and a female asked what he wanted.

"I want to get screwed," said Feldman.

"Okay, mister, but this is a private club," said the woman, "slip fifty bucks as an initiation fee through the mail slot."

Feldman did, and the panel closed. Ten minutes passed and nothing happened. He began to pound on the door and the panel slid open. "Hey," exclaimed the salesman, "I want to get screwed!"

"What," said the woman, "again?"

* * *

A traveling salesman was put up for the night by an elderly farmer who had only one bed. In the middle of the night the old man woke up and began shouting "Bring me a woman! I've gotta have a woman! Look at that erection! I haven't had a stiff one in 20 years!"

"Take it easy, old fella," soothed the salesman. "You don't need a woman. That's some erection, all right, but it isn't yours—it's mine!"

* * *

Stan Kozlowski, the talented Texas tall tales teller, gets titters with this joyful jibe:

Denise had an appointment with an optometrist to have her eyes examined.

On her way to his office, she stopped in a shoe store and began to try on several pairs of shoes. As the clerk bent over to measure her foot, Denise, who was very nearsighted, saw the clerk's bald head and thought it was her bare knee showing. She quickly pulled her skirt over it.

"Damn it," shouted the clerk, "There goes that light fuse again!"

Said a shoe clerk in accents most daring,
"Miss, I'm sharing the view you are airing.
  "A pink pump would suit,
  "Or a brown fur-trimmed boot
"Would look cute with the pants you're
not wearing."

* * *

Diane DuParque, the comely computer service coordinator, came up with this cackler:

One evening while covering her South Carolina territory, Angela's car ran out of gas. A farmer put her up for the night in his son's room. Very quickly she discovered the boy knew nothing about making love. Angela tried to explain, but Junior was totally unfamiliar with the sport. She was strongly attracted to the backward Adonis, however, and she offered him twenty dollars if he would play a game with her.

"Now," she instructed, after she had him where she wanted him. "Go up. Now go down. Now go up. Now go down."

Junior rolled back to his side of the bed. "Here's your twenty dollars back, lady," he said. "You don't know what the hell you want."

* * *

TRAVELING MAN'S TOAST

*Here's to the kisses you've
snatched and vice versa*

Arlene, a saleslady, was on her way to Atlanta when the car broke down. Always resourceful, she trudged to a farmhouse and asked to stay overnight. The farmer explained that she'd have to sleep with his son, Clem.

They went to Clem's room, and he was still awake. "How come you're not sleeping?" asked the farmer.

" 'Cause I didn't have my warm milk yet," said the strapping eighteen-year old.

"This here lady's stayin' with us tonight," said the farmer. "She'll have to sleep with you, son!"

Arlene undressed and got into bed with the boy. In a few minutes she began teaching him fancy aspects of lovemaking. Pretty soon she smiled and said, "Well, Clem, now's your chance."

So he got out of bed and drank his warm milk.

* * *

Bleiffer, a traveling salesman, took out a girl from a small Midwestern town. After dinner, they parked on a deserted road and climbed into the back seat. He didn't have a condom, so he used a silk handkerchief. A few years later Bleiffer was passing through the same town and saw a little boy who looked exactly like himself. "Well, you're a fine little fellow," said the salesman.

"I ought to be," said the boy. "Mama says I was strained through a silk handkerchief."

* * *

·

On his way to a Cleveland sales conference, Geoffrey got lost in a snowstorm. He came to a farmhouse and asked if he could rent a room for the night. The farmer told him he could sleep with his son.

Geoffrey entered the son's room, threw his clothes on a chair and hopped into bed. Then he noticed the boy kneeling beside the bed, his head bowed. Geoffrey felt slightly ashamed to be reminded by a youngster to say his prayers. He got out of bed and knelt down, on the opposite side from the boy.

"Mister, you're gonna get in trouble with Pop," said the boy. "The pot's on this side!"

FALSIE SALESMAN

A fuller bust man

* * *

Lyle was in Miami and feeling strongly in need of feminine companionship. He struck up a conversation with the hotel bartender, who advised, "That blonde in the corner booth is available and reasonable. She expects to be taken out for dinner."

Lyle made contact, and they went off together to a very expensive restaurant, where she ordered practically everything on the menu. "Do you always eat this much?" asked Lyle, thinking of the dent in his expense account.

"Oh, no," she replied, "only when I'm un-well."

* * *

A traveling salesman made the sad mistake of picking up a hitchhiker who repaid him by taking his car, clothes, and everything he had at gunpoint. To add insult to injury, the crook left the salesman in the heat of the lonely highway, stark naked, bent over, his wrists tied to his ankles. The poor man looked like a plucked turkey.

Suddenly, a huge trailer truck stopped and out stepped a burly driver. The salesman explained what happened. The trucker smiled, and, loosening his belt, said, "Well, buddy, I guess this just ain't your day!"

A traveling salesman bragged to a farmer that he knew two hundred positions for intercourse. "Bet I got one you don't know," said the farmer.

He led the salesman out to a hay-rig with a bottomless bushel basket attached to the rope. "I put the hired girl in the basket with her dress up," explained the farmer. "Then I lay underneath and pull the basket up and lower her down."

"But why go to all that trouble?" asked the salesman.

"Cause when I want to jazz—I spin it!"

* * *

Tesler's car broke down one evening on a lonely road. He went up to the only farmhouse in sight, and when the farmer came to the door, he asked, "Can you put me up for the night?"

"I suppose I can," said the farmer. "But you'll have to share a room with my young son."

"How do you like that?" said the salesman, "I'm in the wrong joke."

* * *

They buried a salesman named Phipps,
Who married on one of his trips.
    A widow named Block
    Then died of the shock
When she found there were five little chips.

69

Scene: Hotel room. Sidney, a silk sales-man, and the hotel maid are sitting on the bed in a warm embrace. The telephone rings. Reluctantly, Sidney picks up the receiver.

Sidney: (*into phone*) "Hello. What's that? . . . My wife is on her way up? But . . . Hello? Hello!"

Maid: (*angrily*) "Your wife? You didn't tell me you were married."

Sidney: "But . . ."

Maid: (*interrupting*) "When your wife comes in, she'll find me in your bed with no clothes on. (*She gets under the covers and removes all her clothes.*) Then you'll know better next time."

Sidney: But . . . (*Phone rings. He picks up the receiver.*) "Hello, What's that? . . . The other call was a mistake? . . . Oh, I see, you rang the wrong room." (*Hangs up.*)

Maid: "But . . ."

Sidney: (*removing trousers*) "Okay, honey, move over."

* * *

Seymour propositioned the new waitress. "Okay," she replied. "I'll have sex with you if you'll guarantee that lights will flash and bells will ring."

So Seymour screwed her on top of the pinball machine.

Parker stopped at a farmhouse one evening and asked to stay for the night.

"I could let you sleep with my daughter," said the farmer, "if you promise not to bother her."

The salesman agreed. After dinner Parker was led to the room. He undressed in the dark, slipped into bed, and felt the farmer's daughter at his side.

The next morning he asked for his bill.

"It'll just be $10, since you had to share the bed," said the farmer.

"Your daughter was very cold," said the salesman.

"Yes, I know," said the farmer. "We're gonna bury her today."

* * *

SALESMAN'S SOPHISTRY

Girls are like pianos. When they're not upright, they're grand.

* * *

"Tuckerman is the slickest salesman in the world."

"How do you know?"

"He actually made his wife feel sorry for the poor girl who lost her bra and panties in his car."

* * *

Klaman sold silk stockings. One night in a Chicago restaurant he became friendly with his waitress, Carol, a young lady working her way through college. "How about us getting together?" he asked.

"You wouldn't enjoy it," Carol replied. "I'm a lousy lay. I'm only interested in getting my engineering degree."

"Let's give it a chance," persisted Klaman, "I won't complain."

"No!" she refused.

Then he opened his box of samples and said, "See these top-grade silk stockings? Give me half an hour, and you can have two dozen of them. What's more, I'll bet you'll enjoy it."

"Okay," she agreed, "if that's the way you want it."

Later that night, they went to his room, and he found her absolutely fantastic in bed. She wiggled and squirmed and contorted beautifully.

"You were wrong," he said, "I can see you really enjoyed it."

"No," said the coed. "I was just trying on the stockings!"

* * *

Carnal Collegians

Brian had enjoyed his sophomore sexpot to the fullest and was preparing to slip out of bed. Suddenly the girl whispered in his ear.

"A contribution?" he exclaimed. "What the hell are you—a prostitute masquerading as a college girl?"

"No, dear," she replied, "a business major."

* * *

Brad and Irene, Washington State seniors, were returning from a canoe ride. As they pulled up in front of her sorority house he said, "Wasn't it lovely out there on the lake?"

With a sigh Irene replied, "It's lovely any-place."

There was a young coed from Kent,
Who claimed not to know what they meant,
When men asked her age.
She'd reply in a rage,
"My age is the age of consent."

* * *

The Dean of Women called in a Chicago coed to her office. "Your housemother tells me that you smoke pot, take LSD and have made love to every boy on campus," exclaimed the woman. "Don't you know what good, clean fun is?"

"No," said the coed, "what good is it?"

* * *

The girls in a small North Carolina college town where men are few have slumber parties where they satisfy each other with a candle. One of the girls smuggled in her handsome cousin disguised as a woman, and three girls got pregnant.

"But how could it have happened?" asked one girl's father.

"I don't know, Papa. The darned old candle must have melted!"

* * *

COLLEGE NYMPHOMANIAC

A go-go-go-go girl

Courtland was telling a fraternity brother about his date with Cassie, the campus homecoming queen. He had taken her to an amusement park.

"I took Cassie through the Tunnel of Love," he said. "Gee, it sure is wonderful. That place is just made for love. A real nice boat, the pleasant sound of lapping water. Darkness. Everything peaceful and quiet."

"Did Cassie enjoy it too?" he was asked.

"I don't know," complained Courtland, "we couldn't get seats together."

* * *

Dan and Carla were strolling hand in hand across the Michigan campus, talking about their relationship. "I don't mind having your mother live with us," said Dan, "but I really wish she'd wait until we get married."

* * *

Did you hear about the Columbia coed who graduated Magna Cum Loaded?

* * *

Student: I want a nice room for me and my wife.
Clerk: Okay, just sign the register. Anything else?
Student: Yeah, give me a pack of cigarettes.
Clerk: What brand?
Student: (turning to girl) What kind of cigarettes do you smoke, babe?

Bragged an innocent coed, Miss Chow,
"I *don't* . . . I don't even know how!"
The Dean of Men caught her,
And oh! What he taught her!
She can't get enough of it now.

* * *

Oliver pulled into the campus lover's lane that was crowded with other cars. "It's lovely out here tonight," sighed his date. "Just listen to the crickets."

"Those aren't crickets," said Oliver, "they're zippers!"

* * *

TEN TOES

*An old, but still very popular game
on campus. The girls all play with
ten toes up, the boys all play with
ten toes down*

* * *

Norman picked up Madeline at the dorm and took her for a drive. They came to a quiet spot out in the country and the car stopped.

"Out of gas," said Norman.

Madeline picked up her purse, opened it and pulled out a bottle.

"Wow!" exclaimed Norman. "You've got a whole pint—what kind is it?"

"Gasoline," replied the girl.

Coed: I'm worried about this short skirt. I'm afraid if I bend over, someone might see my underwear. (Bending over) There, can you see my panties?

Milt: No.

Coed: Well, I'll bend over a little farther. There—can you see them now?

Milt: No, but I think you'd better put some on!

* * *

Oh, Ralph, let's not park here
Oh, Ralph, let's not park
Oh, Ralph, let's not
Oh, Ralph, let's
Oh, Ralph
Oh!

* * *

Jeffrey, a USC senior, was cruising around Hollywood in his Jaguar XKE when he spotted Eve, a pretty redhead, waiting for a bus. He stopped at the curb, asked if she wanted a lift, and Eve accepted. As she seated herself, Eve shyly told him that she was a witch and could turn him into anything she desired.

"Go ahead and try," he laughed.

Leaning over, Eve whispered something in his ear. And sure, enough, he turned into a motel.

* * *

Jim Hibbs, the dynamic Dixon Cadillac Service Manager, donated this delightful doozy:

Late at night a police officer was checking cars on a quiet street in Westwood. In one he saw a UCLA senior reading a book in the front seat and a frosh co-ed knitting in the back seat.

Policeman: What are you doing here?

Senior: Can't you see, reading a book.

Policeman: How old are you?

Senior: Twenty.

Policeman: What is she doing in the back?

Senior: Can't you see? Knitting.

Policeman: How old is she?

Senior: (Looking at watch) In eleven minutes she will be eighteen.

Did you hear about the Iowa State coed who finally got fed up with her shy boyfriend's fumbling advances and decided to put him in her place?

* * *

At the University of New Mexico the battle was on to select someone for the Miss Albuquerque beauty contest. However, Olivia won by a unamimous vote. She was the only contestant who could get all those letters across her chest.

* * *

A student from dear old Bryn Mawr
Committed a dreadful faux pas.
   She loosened a stay
   In her new decolleté,
Exposing her je ne sais quoi.

* * *

STRAPLESS EVENING GOWN

A bust truster

* * *

Home on a semester break from Vanderbilt, soph Sandy advised her younger sister, "You can never tell about school athletes. Either they're so slow you want to scream, or so fast you have to."

* * *

Barbara and Rita, two Pennsylvania coeds, were chatting at the student center. "What were you doing until three o'clock in the morning?" asked Barbara.

"Oh, I learned a new game," replied Rita. "It's called backgammon. First he went down on me, then I went down on him. Then he got up on top of me, then I got on top of him. Then . . ."

"Wait a second! That's backgammon? Who taught you how to play it?"

"My new boyfriend!"

* * *

Dolores, a Texas Tech junior, daintily lifted her skirt to show Ernie the new panties she had just bought at Neiman-Marcus in Dallas.

"They're really nice," said Ernie. "Are they nylon?"

"No," said Dolores, "they're not nylon, they're silk."

"But," said Ernie, "if they're silk, aren't they apt to run?"

"It all depends," said the coed, "on who's chasing them."

* * *

"Do you smoke after sex?" asked the campus grid star.

"I really don't know," replied the pretty cheerleader. "I've never looked to see."

* * *

"I'll tell you," smiled prom chairman Mose,
"Why Peggy's the prom queen I chose:
  She's as cheerfully free
  As the wind on the sea—
And besides, like the wind, Peggy blows!"

* * *

Professor Kranz was disturbed over the poor marks his class had made in the recent exam. He called several students to his desk, "Mr. Cramer, why didn't you prepare for your exam?"

"I was holding hands with a girl last night, sir," said the student.

"You are suspended for two days," snapped the professor. "And Mr. Gibson, why didn't you study for your exam?"

"Eh, I was playing post office all of last night."

"Suspended for one week," said the prof. "And . . . here, Mr. Shuman, where are you going?"

"So long, professor," said Shuman, "See you next term."

* * *

INTRA-UTERINE DEVICE

A box spring

* * *

Did you hear about the coed who thought she was a robot because she was made by a scientist?

* * *

One morning the medical professor said to his class, "What would you do if a child was born without a penis?"

"Well," quipped one of the students, "I'd wait until she's sixteen, and then *give* her one!"

* * *

Did you hear about the absent-minded professor exhibitionist who was arrested for exposing his watchamacallit?

* * *

The biology professor pointed to Miss Ellison and asked, "What part of the human anatomy enlarges to about 10 times its normal size during periods of emotion or excitement?"

"I . . . Eh, refuse to answer that question," she stammered, her face beet red.

Miss Evans was asked the same question and answered, correctly, "The pupil of the eye."

"Miss Ellison," said the prof, "your refusal to answer the question leads me to three conclusions: One, you didn't study last night's assignment; two, you have a dirty mind; and three, your marriage will be a tremendous disappointment."

* * *

There was a young coed from Dover
Whose passion was such that it drove her
    To cry, when you came,
    "Oh, Gosh, what a shame!
"Well, we'll just have to start up all over."

Rosalie Brody Feder, the pretty New York publicist, came up with this pleasing piece of persiflage:

Bitsy, a Washington State sophomore, spent Easter vacation in San Francisco where she met Quentin, a young painter. Bitsy wound up her holiday with many fond memories.

A few months later the coed returned to the Bay City with her mother and they attended an exhibition of Quentin's paintings. As they approached an extremely provocative nude, Bitsy's mom noticed that the canvas bore an amazing resemblance to her daughter.

"Bitsy," she gasped, "that painting looks exactly like you. Don't tell me you've been posing in the nude!"

"Of course not, Mother," said the girl, "H-he must have painted it from memory."

Nathaniel, home for Christmas vacation, was reading in the family room. His father addressed him rather gruffly, "What are you majoring in?"

"Ecology and sexology."

"Ecology and sexology. How do you expect to make a living with those majors? I don't object to ecology, but sexology! For that nonsense, I'm paying $10,000 a year!"

Nathaniel and his father got into an argument, and soon the boy ran upstairs to his room and slammed the door.

His mother, who had overheard everything, was unhappy because of the quarrel. She tiptoed up the stairs and quietly opened Nathaniel's door. There he lay on the bed masturbating.

"Darling," she pleaded, "when you finish your homework, please go down and make up with papa!"

* * *

CAMPUS MARATHON

A hit-the-sack race

* * *

"Oh, I just had a wonderful time," cooed the California coed to her mother. "Everybody said that Sherwood and I were the cutest couple on the floor."

"Isn't that nice," said her mother. "There's nothing quite like a sorority dance."

"Oh, we weren't at the dance. Sherwood took me to a pajama party!"

* * *

Ross ran into Stephen, his fraternity brother, at the Grog Shop.

"Did you follow my advice about kissing your date when she least expected it?"

"Oh, hell," said Stephen, holding his swollen eye, "I thought you said where."

* * *

Diane and Ivana, two Syracuse sorority sisters, were babbling over a double malt, "How did you like the bridge party that the Sigs threw last night?" asked Diane.

"Fine," answered Ivana, "until the campus cops came and looked under the bridge."

* * *

Paula, a Pittsburgh drama major, had a pair of panties tattooed on her hips. When the tattooer asked for $50, she complained, "But you tattooed a pair of panties just like this for my sorority sister for only $25."

"Yes," said the tattooer, "but I went into the hole on that job."

* * *

"Austerity now is the fashion,"
Remarked a young coed with passion.
Then she glanced at the bed,
And quietly said,
"There's one thing no nation can ration."

The lovable jester Jay Lester tells about sorority sisters, Vera and Hortense who were gabbing at the student club. The subject was men, and Hortense, a not very attractive miss, was all excited.

"I tell you," she said, "he's the only guy in my whole life who's made me feel this way. Oh, the touch of his hand, the sound of his voice, the . . ."

"You sure sound pretty far gone on him," said Vera.

"Oh, yes," said Hortense. "This time it's the real thing—sex."

* * *

Ed: It's so dark I can't see my hand in front of my face.
Coed: Don't worry. I know where it is.

* * *

Anna attended a junior college but still lived at home. One evening she asked her father, "Any calls, Dad?"

"Yeah," he replied "someone named Charlie called and asked to speak to 'Hot Lips.'" Later a Lenny, then an Albert, and finally a fellow named Greg phoned and they too wanted to speak to 'Hot Lips.' Anna, I gotta ask you a very serious question."

"Yes, Dad?"

"Have you been smoking?"

The college kids had made love all night in a motel near the campus, and now they lay in a blissful embrace.

After a few minutes there came a shy whisper, "Oh, Edward, will you always love me the way you did tonight?"

"Of course, my darling," said Edward.

"Will you always love my kissing-sweet lips, my cornsilk hair, the fragrance of my velvet skin, and the way my limpid blue-green eyes wrinkle when I laugh?"

"How could I do anything else, sweetheart?" yawned Edward.

"Will you always adore my firm belly, my slender legs, the sensuousness of my juice . . ."

"Yes! Yes!" snapped Edward. "Now will you let me get some sleep, Bruce?"

* * *

Show Biz Baubles

"I've got a great client I can't get placed at any of the studios," moaned a Hollywood agent.

"Maybe I can help you," said another ten-percenter, "What's your client like?"

"Got a build like Bo Derek, sings like Barbra Streisand, and can act like Marsha Mason!" raved the first agent.

"Well, you shouldn't have any trouble placing her," assured his friend.

"Her?!" exploded the agent. "It's a *him*!"

* * *

Two producers met at the Brown Derby. "How's your new film going?" asked one.

"The picture was a runaway success." replied the second.

"Really?"

"Yeah. The director ran away with the studio's money, and the two male stars ran away with each other."

91

HOLLYWOOD

Where ambitious young actresses
go to make love under the stars.

* * *

Bobbi Bresee, the film capital's newest glamour girl, gets giggles with this goofy gag:

A movie director began ranting about the cast's lack of acting ability. In his rage he even accused them of lacking moral character. Suddenly, the young leading lady stalked off the set.

The next day she threw a document at the director.

"What's this?" he asked.

"A medical certificate attesting to my virginity," she sneered.

"But it's no good," said the director. "It's dated yesterday!"

* * *

Did you hear about the pretty Mexican girl who told the movie producer that she wanted to be a Sollywood harlot?

* * *

There's a starlet who's still in her teens,
Who's adept at removing her jeans.
    And in X-rated flicks
    So accomplished with pricks
That she steals all the pictures' obscenes.

A shapely starlet about to go for an interview with a producer was warned by her girlfriend, "Listen, honey, I don't want to upset you, but this guy's got a bad reputation with women. If he gets you alone in his office, he's liable to rip the dress right off your back!"

"Thanks for the warning," said the starlet. "I'll go change into an old one."

* * *

A rising young movie starlet arrived home after a hard day in front of the cameras and found five of her admirers waiting for her.

"Look, guys," she said, "I've had a rough day. Been working since dawn. I'm knocked out. So one of you will have to leave."

* * *

MODERN MOVIE RATINGS

G The hero gets the girl.
R The bad guy gets the girl.
X Everybody gets the girl.

* * *

A glamorous movie queen just arrived by oceanliner and was being interviewed. "I understand," said the reporter, "you were courted by many European noblemen during your four weeks abroad."

"That's right, honey," she replied smiling. "I managed to make every second count."

After six months of auditioning for various producers, Adele finally landed a part in a western.

The first day she was thrown off her horse. The next day, she had to jump from a balcony, her clothes on fire, into a water tank and nearly drowned. On the third day, she was roughed up by a cow hand and the director reshot the scene five times. Then, the next day a crazed bull chased her around the corral for ten minutes before they could divert the animal.

Wearily, she limped into the producer's office. "Listen," said Adele, "who do I have to sleep with to get out of this picture?"

* * *

Did you hear about the porno actress who is quitting films?

She doesn't like some of the parts she's been asked to play with.

* * *

The young actress was complaining to her agent. "I'm an artist and I'll do anything to get a really good part," she said, "but there are limits, you know."

"Is that why you turned down the walk on part Stanley Lasfinkel offered you in his new picture?"

"That's right. A lousy part like that could ruin my whole career."

"What did you do when Stanley offered it to you?"

"I laughed right in his balls."

Did you hear about the high-salaried movie director who was always trying to make a little extra?

* * *

An aging film actor took a young starlet for his fifth wife, and they spent several weeks in the mountains on their honeymoon.

Upon his return to Hollywood he met a movie gossip columnist.

"Well," said the columnist, "if it isn't Beverly Hills' gift to the panting females! And all by himself, too! I suppose the little woman is home nursing her disappointment."

"You know a remark like that is not only untrue, but it hurts me to the quick." replied the actor. "And I want you to be the first to know that right now I've got the sorest quick in Hollywood!"

* * *

TV Emcee: How many husbands have you had?
Movie Star: Should I count my own?

* * *

The sugar daddy handed the beautiful Vegas chorus girl a gorgeous diamond clip backstage.

"Oh," she beamed. "I'm going on in a minute. Can I wear it now?"

"Certainly, my dear," he leered. "You may wear it until the end of the act."

Jackie Maitland, the hilarious off-hour Rockers Records star, donated this ribald rib-tickler:

A big Las Vegas hotel planned a new version of their hit Hollywood musical revue. The dance director was auditioning a lovely chorus cutie. "All right," he said, "learn to walk straight. Toss your head back and hold your breast out!"

"Okay," she replied. "Which one?"

Says a showgirl who works at the Lido,
"I've developed a flexible credo:
    I support women's rights,
    But there are, frankly, nights
When the lib that I flaunt is libido."

*   *   *

Did you hear about the Las Vegas go-go dancer who was rushed to the hospital?
She caught a strip-de-carcass infection.

*   *   *

The captain of a Vegas chorus girl line received this note from a high roller. It said, "Please do me the honor of sharing a champagne supper with me in my suite tonight, for I have long worshipped you from afar. You are the only girl for me.

"P.S.: If you are busy tonight, please pass this note to the girl next to you."

*   *   *

Jerry Snyder, the Santa Monica condo king, gets giggles with this jolly jest:
Marla the showgirl returned from her honeymoon with the amorous old millionaire. She explained to her friend, "I just happened to have the combination that opened his safe: 38-24-34."

*   *   *

1st Chorine: I was never so insulted in my life!

2nd Chorine: What did the louse do?

1st Chorine: He drove me straight home!

* * *

Rick had a steady role on a sit-com. One afternoon he came home unexpectedly and found his wife in bed with another actor. He snapped, "What are you doing?"

"Well," said the other ham, "I've got a part in General Hospital, a TV movie. . . ."

* * *

A Broadway actress, notorious for her many romances, was being interviewed backstage by a newspaperman. "Are you engaged to the man you've been seen with around town at the night spots?"

"That's the trouble with you reporters," she said sharply. "A girl can't go to bed with a man without somebody saying she's engaged to him."

* * *

For her Hamlet in drag, actress Hubb
Learned her lines while immersed in the tub.
    Using Method a bit,
    She would finger her clit
As she memorized, "Ah, there's the rub!"

Jennifer, Penelope and Aileen, three chorus girls, were undressing. Jennifer had the impression of a Y on her abdomen and explained that her sweetheart was a Yale man who forgot to remove his belt.

Penelope had an H, for Harvard.

On Aileen's stomach was an F.

"Your boyfriend goes to Fordham?" asked Jennifer.

"No, he's a Fire Chief," replied Aileen. "He just forgot to take off his hat."

* * *

There was a young dancer from Ealing,
Who performed with such exquisite feeling,
    That for miles all around,
    There was nary a sound
Save for fly-buttons hitting the ceiling.

* * *

Dick Howard, the top TV theatrical rep, tells this whimsical tail-wagger:

Biff hadn't had a part for months and was forced to work as a waiter.

One night, he came home and found his wife sobbing, with bruises on her face and her dress in shreds.

"What happened?"

"Your agent came here looking for you," she sobbed. "And he . . . he raped me . . . and beat me . . ."

"My agent?"

"Yes!"

"Has he got a part for me?"

Maude and Jeannie, two New York actresses, were lunching at Schraffts.

"In my last four shows," complained Maude, "I've played nothing but prostitutes, alcoholics and nymphos."

"Yes, it's a shame," agreed Jeannie, "This insidious typecasting is ruining the American stage."

* * *

A famous stage actor got married, and the next morning he and the bride were sharing their first breakfast. "Darling," she said, "I should have told you before. I suffer from asthma."

"Thank heavens," said the thespian, blowing her a kiss, "and all the time I thought you were hissing me."

* * *

Basil and Lionel, two retired actors, were reminiscing about their days on Broadway.

"I'll never forget the leading lady who treated me to my first sexual encounter," said Basil. "I can still hear the '*slap, slap, sigh,*' as our bare bellies met and parted."

"I, too, had a partner who put out," retorted Lionel. "Oh, the thrill of that '*clap, clap, whistle,*' when her palpitating flesh made contact with mine."

"Say," asked Basil, "how did you make it go '*clap, clap, whistle*'?"

"We didn't," said the other actor, "those were the sounds of applause from the audience."

Stormy Wynd, the New York nightclub stripper, was sitting in the Harry Brine Theatrical Agency office. "Honey," said the agent, "I got a great gig for you up in Yonkers. The Blue Bird Club."

"Are you kidding? I don't wanna work that joint. The audience there is terrible. The guys are like animals. The place is awful."

"Look, sweetie, they need somebody bad. I'll go up with you for the opening and see that everything goes okay."

The next night Stormy Wynd strutted out on the Blue Bird stage and went into her act. The all male audience hooted and howled as she slowly removed each article of her clothing. When she finally got down to her G-string and pasties, two drunks leaped up on the stage.

The men ripped off her costume and while one sat on her face, the other raped her. Then they changed places. The joint went wild.

Thirty minutes later, Harry Brine rushed into her dressing room, shouting, "Stormy, that was sensational! What a finish!"

"What!" snapped the stripper. "Did you hear how lousy that band was?"

Actor: Honey, don't you know it's bad luck to whistle in a dressing room?

Actress: Maybe so, but with your reputation I want anyone listening to know I am having normal sex.

* * *

A world-famous repertory company was giving a performance in a small western town. When the hero cried his tragic lines, "What shall I do with her body?" a voice from the balcony shouted. "Screw it before it gets cold!"

At the next performance the sheriff was stationed down front of the balcony with two guns to prevent a similar disturbance. The danger point safely passed, but in the following scene the hero asked the heroine, "What can be sweeter than your lips? What can be softer than your heart?"

The sheriff jumped up and shouted, "I'll shoot the first son-of-a-bitch that answers that!"

* * *

Thirty days hath September
April, June and November.
All the rest have thirty-one
Except Dolly Parton, who has a perfect forty-six.

* * *

Walcot stuttered badly. One evening at a party he was introduced to a beautiful actress. Walcot became so tongue-tied she gave him pencil and paper to write down what he had to say.

"I've had this experience before," said the actress to the hostess. "Whenever men see me, their tongues get so hard they can't talk."

* * *

A hot-blooded actress named Fawn,
Could make love from the dusk 'till the dawn,
    She let no one slip past,
    But took on the whole cast,
'Cause she heard that the show must go on.

* * *

After the evening performance, a ham actor went to a bawdy house and retired to the room of a pretty blonde. As he disrobed, she eyed his rather well-endowed manhood and exclaimed, "Wow!"

"Don't get carried away, my dear," said the thespian, "we have come to bury Caesar, not to praise him."

* * *

BELLY DANCER'S AGENT

An abdominal showman

* * *

An actor showed up at his agent's office sporting a black eye. "How'd you get that shiner?" asked the ten percenter.

"From one of the dancer's at the opening night party," said the thespian. "I kissed her."

"What's wrong with that?" asked the agent.

"Well," said the actor, "she was in the middle of a cartwheel at the time."

* * *

Did you hear about the aging playwright who, no matter how hard he tried, could never get beyond the first act?

* * *

Tallulah Bankhead, at a Hollywood cocktail party, overheard an obnoxious young movie actress bragging about being chaste. "In fact," declared the starlet, "I happen to be the only girl in this town who still has her cherry!"

"But dahling!" clucked Tallulah, "doesn't it get in your way when you're screwing?"

* * *

* * *

Robin Williams, perhaps the most keen-witted comic to ever make an audience howl, was quoted as saying, "Many a starlet who is trying to make it to the top usually wears clothes that don't."

* * *

Milton Berle took George Burns aside at a Hollywood benefit. "Now that you're a movie star again, I hear the women swoon over you."

"I have very faithful fans," answered the octogenerian comedian, "but when they swoon now, it takes them longer to get up."

* * *

Later in the evening George said to Berle, "You've been a star a long time. Why don't you retire?"

"I'm ten years younger than you are," Berle answered. "Why don't *you* retire?"

"I can't quit now," replied Burns, "I'm all booked up."

"How can *I* quit?" said Milton. "I still have 300 glossy pictures and $200 worth of makeup left."

* * *

Bob Williams, the handsome Hollywood video producer, convulses cohorts with this shrewdie:

Cecil B. DeMille got to heaven and was welcomed by St. Peter. "You just can't know how happy we are that you've joined us. We want you to direct a big picture for us."

"Really? What have you got lined up?"

"Well, Beethoven is doing the music, Shakespeare has written the script, Michelangelo has created the sets, and Thomas Edison will be on the camera."

"Sounds good," said DeMille. "Who's the star?"

"Well," said St. Peter, "God has this girl . . ."

* * *

Merry Midgets

Danny stood two feet four inches tall. He just returned from his vacation at a California Nude Ranch. "How was it?" asked a friend.

"At first I thought I'd been skyjacked to Havana," replied Danny. "Everybody in the joint looked like Fidel Castro."

* * *

Little Claude married a woman over six feet tall. When he returned from his honeymoon, his friends cornered him. "How are you getting on?" they asked.

"I'm getting on fine," he said, "but I have no one to talk to."

San Diego opened a drive-in restaurant for foreign sports cars. They just hired the waitresses —26 midgets!

* * *

Mrs. Rizutto was suing for a divorce.

"Surely, you knew your husband was a midget when you married him," questioned the judge. "Why do you want to leave him? Didn't you anticipate the problems this marriage would encounter?"

"Your honor," sobbed the woman, "Everything was wonderful, except for sex."

"What has his being a midget got to do with sex?" asked the jurist.

"Well," she replied, "when we're nose to nose, his toes are in it, when we're toes to toes, his nose is in it, and when he's in it, he disappears altogether, and oh, your honor, I get so lonely!"

* * *

A foolhardy midget named Fisher
Stuck his digit in Fat Lady's fissure.
  Her labial snap
  Caught him in a trap
Now they're fishing the fissure for Fisher.

* * *

Did you hear about the midget who entered a dancing contest in a nudist colony and was clubbed to death?

110

Nothing in the world could stop Hilliard (eight feet, three inches), the circus giant, from marrying Melissa (three feet, seven inches), the lady midget. He was nuts over her!

* * *

Girls go ape over Matthew the midget,
Who makes out with a minuscule digit.
   For you see when you bang,
    'Tain't the size of your whang;
What girls dig in a fug's how you fidget.

* * *

Did you hear about the Ft. Lauderdale delicatessen owner hiring midget waiters so his sandwiches would look bigger?

* * *

A midget fortune teller escaped from jail. The next day the headlines read, ''Small Medium at Large.''

* * *

Morty, the midget singing star, married a tall Las Vegas showgirl. On their honeymoon they looked high and low for each other!

DEMIJOHN

A rest room for midgets

* * *

Bud Potter, the bubbling Los Angeles bank manager, charms customers with this corker:

Little Rachel went to a doctor and complained that she had a terrible pain in her groin whenever it rained or snowed.

"Come back next time the weather is inclement," said the doctor.

Three days later, Rachel returned during a snowstorm. The doctor had her lie down for five seconds, then told her to get back on her feet and walk around a bit. "Still have the pain in your groin?" he inquired.

"No, I feel fine," she answered. "What did you do?"

"Oh," he replied, "I just cut four inches off the top of your galoshes."

The midget was accused of using a bucket to rape a six foot tall fat woman. His lawyer stood him on a bucket and showed, how, with one kick, the woman could have knocked over both the bucket and him.

The midget was acquitted, but the judge still had his doubts. He took him aside and said, "It's all over now and you can't be tried twice, but I know damn well you did it. How?"

The midget winked. "The bucket."

"But didn't your lawyer . . . couldn't the woman . . . ?"

"I didn't stand on it," said the midget, "I put it over her head and swung from the handle."

* * *

A nudist resort at Benares
Took a midget in all unawares.
    But he made members weep
    For he just couldn't keep
His nose out of private affairs.

MIDGET CIRCUMCISION

Tiny trim

At his Little People Golf Tournament, Billy Barty, America's most beloved shorter person, kidded about his size.

"On my wedding night I got so drunk I attacked the bride on top of the wedding cake."

A Florida reporter knocked on the door of the circus midget who was to be interviewed. He was astonished when a man six feet tall answered the door.

"Is this the residence of Tom Thumb?"

"I'm Tom Thumb, it's my day off."

* * *

Did you hear about the midget in the side show who raped the giant woman?

The strong man put him up to it.

* * *

A large Midwestern city has agreed to give rental units gratis to midgets.

They will be called stay free mini-pads!

* * *

One of New York's biggest nightclubs just announced it is going to introduce a new act: A midget stripteaser. She'll entertain the customers who are under the tables.

* * *

Suzanne was furious when she came home unexpectedly and caught her husband Mervyn in bed with a female midget. "You promised me two weeks ago that you'd never cheat on me again," she shouted.

"But, honey," said Mervyn, "can't you see? I'm tapering off!"

The driver had a long one and it was getting close to midnight. Travis, a huge trucker, coming through Ohio parked his big rig and went into a bar to relax. After a few beers, Travis headed for the men's room.

As he was standing at the urinal he glanced over at a midget who was using the urinal next to his. Travis stared in amazement at the midget's extra plumbing. "Good Gawrsh, man!" the trucker stammered. "How long is that when it's *on*, man?"

"Hell," said the little guy. "I've never found out. I always pass out from the lack of blood."

* * *

FUNNY FAIRIES

Thaddeus strolled into a Western Union office and asked the operator, "Is it true that you telegraph flowers anywhere?"

"Of course," she said.

"Wonderful!" shouted Thaddeus, "send me to New York. I'm a pansy!"

* * *

How did you feel when you first discovered you were a homosexual?

It was quite a blow.

* * *

An alligator walked into the men's department of Bonwit Teller. Naturally, the manager was shocked. He rushed up to the reptile and said, "Can I help you?"

"Yes," said the alligator, "do you have any shirts with the little faggot on the pocket?"

Two grandmothers, Mrs. Schwartz and Mrs. Berkowitz, were walking down Lexington Avenue one afternoon. At 61st Street, they were nearly swept off the sidewalk by a brace of squealing queens.

"You know," said Mrs. Schwartz, "if I had my way, all those people would be taken out somewhere and shot."

"But sweetheart," said Mrs. Berkowitz, "if they did that, Bloomingdale's would be self-service."

* * *

HOMOSEXUAL

A man's man

* * *

"Isn't it awful about Clarence?"

"What?"

"He got a parking ticket for being fast in the parking lot. The cops caught him doing 69 in his car."

* * *

Did you hear about the gay tattoo artist who had designs on several of the local sailors?

* * *

"Could you kill a man?" asked Stoddard.

"Yes," answered Kenneth. "But it might take weeks and weeks!"

FUNNY VALENTINE

"Alas! Our love can never be
For I'm a he, the same as thee."

* * *

Louis and Samuel were standing near the elevator door. The door opened and the elevator operator asked, "Going down?"

"Certainly not," replied Samuel. "We're just conversing!"

* * *

At San Quentin, two cellmates, Howard and Milo, lay in their bunks, dreaming out loud. "Say," said Howard, "how would you like to have a beautiful pair of lips on yours right now?"

"I'd love it," answered Milo. "Get down here fast."

* * *

What is the favorite song of the Gay Teamsters?

"Queen of the Load."

* * *

"I've read in the Naval history books that in the old days on the high seas there was little fraternization among the crew."

"That's true. Very few of them ever saw each other face-to-face."

Vincent and Lance were sipping cocktails in a bar when an attractive well-built blonde walked by. Vincent didn't even look up, but Lance stared in obvious appreciation, and let out a long whistle.

"Oh," said Vincent, "you're not thinking of going straight, are you?"

"Of course not," replied Lance, "but when I see something like that go by, I sometimes wish I'd been born a lesbian."

An old fairy tale tells of a king who had three marriageable daughters. One day he announced that any prince in the kingdom who could pass the test could marry his choice of the three.

All the princes in the kingdom tried and failed to pass the tests.

Then Prince Charming arrived on his white charger and the king said, "If you pass the test, you can have your choice."

The king explained the tests and Prince Charming went forth into the world. A year later, he came back and told the king of the dragons he had slain, of the fair maidens he had rescued, and of the battles he had fought.

"Son," said the king, "you may have your choice in marriage. Whom do you choose?"

"You!"

The prince and the king were married and lived happily ever after.

I told you it was a fairy tale.

* * *

As Warren crossed at an intersection in San Francisco he was clobbered by a city bus that had run a stop sign. A policeman rushed to the scene, loosened Warren's collar and spotted one of those little metal medical tags on a necklace. It read:

> *I am a masochist.*
> *In case of an accident,*
> *please wait two hours*
> *before calling an ambulance.*

Esmond wasn't a faggot. But people called him a sissy. He was delicate and painfully shy. Everyone in Rock Springs was surprised when his mother finally nagged him into marriage.

After the honeymoon Esmond returned to his job at the gift shop. The delivery boy said to him, "Hey, I'll bet your old lady is pregnant by now."

"I pray that she is," shuddered Esmond. "I don't think I could ever go through with that again."

* * *

GAY MASOCHIST

A sucker for punishment

* * *

Felix was complaining to Derrick, that when he got home the night before he found a man in bed with his wife. "What did you do?" asked Derrick excitedly.

"Do?" said Felix, "the way I slammed the door when I went out, she knew I wasn't pleased!"

* * *

Oscar Wilde (no relation to Larry) once complained to the madam of a Parisian bordello. "I'm bored with every type of girl. Let me have a young boy."

The French madam was indignant. "Monsieur, I will call a gendarme."

"Don't bother, madame. I'm tired of gendarmes too."

Dexter and Quentin, two female impersonators, were discussing their love affairs. "I have a wonderful new boyfriend," said Dexter. "He has the *Star Spangled Banner* tattooed right across his stomach, below his navel!"

"You bitch!" screamed Quentin. "You've been reading my male!"

* * *

Chants from a recent Gay Lib parade:
"Two, four, six, eight
Gays are just as good as straight."

"Two, four, six, eight
How do you know your husband's straight?"

"Two, four, six, eight
Gays don't overpopulate."

* * *

Did you hear about the girl whose fella didn't smoke, swear, or ever make a pass at her?

He also made his own dresses.

* * *

A peeker at peckers named Ray
Hung out at the Y.M.C.A.
    But the dick that he saw
    Was Detective La Fore,
Who hauled the piqued peeker away.

The phone rang in a San Francisco police station. "Hello?" asked the desk sergeant.

"This is Arthur Sumner," said a voice, "I've been attacked and sexually molested by a pervert, right here in my home!"

"What happened, sir?" asked the police officer.

"The man came in the window. I was lying on the bed. When I tried to scream, he put his hand over my mouth. He held a knife to my throat, and undressed so quickly. He was a big, hairy man, more than fifty pounds heavier than me, and hung like . . . Oh! it was terrible. He had an erection, and he knelt on my shoulders and jammed the awful thing down my throat; forced me into fellatio.

"And he kept using obscene language. Finally, he turned me over on my tummy, forcing my legs apart with his knees, and he put that huge thing . . . It must have been twelve inches long, and I don't know how thick . . . into my . . . Just a minute."

"What's the matter, mister?"

"I have to hang up now. He's getting out of the shower."

* * *

Overheard at a Greenwich Village bar:

"Have you ever seen an elephant with Bo Derek braids?"

"Heavens, no!"

"Let me unzip my pants and show you!"

Aubrey, in order to keep up appearances, married a beautiful blonde. One night he discovered her being screwed by her employer on an office couch. Aubrey told his friend, Leopold.

"I hope you got your revenge," lisped Leopold.

"I should say I did," answered Aubrey, "I utterly destroyed the couch."

* * *

Did you hear about the interior decorator who was bruised black and blue in an accident?

He killed himself in depression because he clashed with his drapes.

* * *

There was a young man named Horatio
With a fondness for ice-creamed fellatio.
    He dispensed of his favors
    In thirty-one flavors—
Including his first love, pistachio.

* * *

Rory and Gawaine were flying to Chicago and enjoying a glass of wine. Suddenly, as Rory raised his glass, the plane hit an air pocket and the wine spilled into his lap.

"Oh, my!" cried Gawaine, "let's get you right back to the washroom for a little check-up. I've always wanted to sample *coq au vin*."

Although it had been going on for quite some time Giles never did anything about it. Then one day Giles developed excruciating rectal pain, so he made an appointment with a proctologist. Totally distraught, Giles lay on the examining table as the doctor probed and looked up his anus.

"In all my years of practice, I've never seen anything like this!" declared the doctor. "You've got flowers up your rectum."

"Oh, my," gasped Giles, "look and see if there's a card!"

Sylvester went to his doctor for a physical. After a long examination, the M.D. said, "I have good news and bad news for you. First the good news. In the next few weeks, your penis will grow six inches longer."

"Six inches!" screamed Sylvester. "How marvelous! What's the bad news?"

"It's elephantiasis!" said the doctor.

* * *

BROMO SEXUAL

A fag that fizzes

* * *

Cyril telephoned Ronald in the middle of the night. "My piles are killing me! And I can't get to the doctor till tomorrow morning!"

"Listen," said Ronald, "get some tea leaves and shove them up there. Take a sleeping pill and tomorrow you can go to the doctor!"

Cyril followed his friend's prescription. The next day he rushed to a proctologist, who immediately had him get up on the examination table. The doctor spread his cheeks and muttered, "Hmm, hmmm, hmmm!"

"Something wrong?" cried Cyril.

"No," answered the M.D. "You're going to take a long trip . . . you're going to meet a tall, dark . . ."

* * *

LESBIAN COCKTAIL LOUNGE

A Her-She Bar

* * *

Did you hear about the tough dyke who swaggered into a lesbian bar and offered to lick anyone in the house?

* * *

What's the difference between a butch lesbian and a man who steals food from restaurants?

The restaurant robber snatches eats . . .

* * *

Janet's husband had passed away and she had been living at the home of his younger brother for several weeks. One evening, no longer in control of her emotions, she barged into her brother-in-law's bedroom and pleaded, "Percival, I want you to take off my dress."

The brother-in-law did as she requested.

"Now," Janet continued, "take off my slip."

He did.

"And now," she said, "remove my panties and bra." Percival obeyed.

"Now," she cried, "don't ever let me catch you wearing my things again."

* * *

FRUSTRATION

A transvestite in a nudist colony

* * *

J. Caesar was really a guy—
He was hetero, homo and bi.
 He could have or be had
 By a lass or a lad
Or even by both when he'd try.

* * *

"Hey, Dad, what's a lesbian?
"Ask Mom," replied Pop, "he'll tell you."

* * *

Did you hear about the gay who walked into a Third Avenue Bar, stuck his tongue out at the bartender and told him to put a head on it?

* * *

A Hollywood screenwriter walked into the producer's office and exclaimed, "Boss, we can't make a movie out of this book. It's about lesbians!"

"So who cares," replied the producer. "Rewrite the script and make them Americans!"

* * *

LESBIANS

Insurmountable odds

Did you hear about the transvestite from Yale who wanted to spend his junior year abroad?

* * *

Johnson, Cordova, and Quale were brought before a judge. He said to Johnson, "What's your occupation?"

"I'm a coke-sacker," answered Johnson.

"What's that?" asked the jurist.

"When the coal is put into the furnaces to make steel, it burns and leaves a residue," he explained. "That residue is called coke. I'm the guy who takes the coke and puts it into sacks for shipment. I'm a coke-sacker."

The judge said to the second man, "What's your occupation?"

"I'm a cork-soaker," replied Cordova.

"What in the world is a cork-soaker?" asked the judge.

"Your honor," said Cordova, "in Brazil, where I came from, they take the bark off a cork tree, and in order to process the cork for use, it has to be dipped in a solution for weeks. I'm the one that took the cork and put it into the solution to soak. I'm a cork-soaker."

The judge then turned to Quale.

"And what do you do?"

"Your honor," he lisped, "I'm the real McCoy."

* * *

Swinging Singles

Scott refused to take Lorraine dancing on their first date. "Don't you like dancing?" she asked.

"No," he answered, "it's just screwing set to music."

"Well, what don't you like about that?"

"The music."

* * *

Noel and Charlene were parked in lovers' lane one dark night. Charlene suddenly exclaimed, "Oh . . . oh, please don't do that, or I'll go to pieces."

"Go ahead," panted Noel. "I've got hold of the part I want."

Lil: Do you love me with all your heart and soul?

Phil: Uh huh.

Lil: Do you think I'm the most beautiful girl in the world, bar none?

Phil: Yeah.

Lil: Do you think my lips are like rose petals, my eyes limpid pools, my hair like silk?

Phil: Yup.

Lil: Oh, you say the nicest things.

* * *

The office party was just getting started, and the pretty temporary steno walked up to the company stud. "Hi," she said.

"Hi."

"My name is Elizabeth, but my friends call me Liz."

"Hello Liz," he answered. "My name is Jerry, but I prefer to be called Jericho."

"Jericho?" asked Liz. "Why that?"

"It's just a reciprocal amenity." he grinned.

"Reciprocal amenity?"

"That's right. If a date blows my trumpet, I sure come tumbling down!"

* * *

Gary and Erika adjusting their clothes after a back-seat quickie: "Gosh," said Gary, "if I had known you were still a virgin, I'd have taken more time."

"Well," she rejoined, "if I had known you had more time, I'd have taken off my panty hose."

Bick constantly bragged that no woman could resist his advances. One day his buddies pooled their resources and bet Bick $200 bucks he couldn't make it with a girl named Maxine.

Bick agreed and his friends went to see Maxine. They knew she could really handle this character and she was happy to split the winnings with them. The date was arranged.

Bick wined her, dined her, flattered her. No matter what approach he tried . . . he got nowhere. Finally he drove her home.

Next day, Maxine told the boys to pay off their bet. "But how could you?" they screamed. "You were so goddamn sure of yourself!"

"Listen," she pleaded. "When he threw lines at me, I had smart answers. When he fed me drinks, I tossed them over my shoulder. If he tried to get me in a compromising position, I wiggled my way out!"

"So," asked one of the guys, "what happened?"

"It was on the way home," she confessed. "We were in the car and he said, 'What a beautiful full moon!' Like a dope, I looked! The S.O.B. pushed the button and my head got stuck in the automatic window!"

* * *

Wendell and Cindy were parked in lover's lane. "Honey," he said, "what would you say if I stole a kiss?"

"Well," answered Cindy, "the same thing I'd say to *any* fool who had the chance to swipe a car and only took the hubcaps."

Teenager Tommy returned late from school one afternoon and confessed to his mother that he went to bed with his girlfriend. "I'm disappointed in you," said his mother. "But for telling the truth, you may go to the corner for a milk shake."

The next day, Tommy came home late again, and this time he admitted having sex with one of the neighbors' wives. "Well, at least you're still honest," said his mother, and again he was rewarded with a milk shake.

On the third day the boy announced to both his parents that he had stayed after school and made love to his teacher. His father picked up a frying pan. "Don't hit him," pleaded his mother, "He told us the truth."

"Hit him, hell," said his father. "I'm going to cook the boy a steak. How long do you expect him to keep this up on those lousy milk shakes."

* * *

A passionate kiss is like a spider web . . . it soon leads to the undoing of the fly.

* * *

Nick asked for a little goodnight kiss, but she rebuffed him with, "I don't do that sort of thing on my first date."

"Well," he replied, "how about on your last?"

* * *

Danny went into the drugstore and asked for a box of rubbers.

"What color?" inquired the druggist.

"What color?" asked Danny. "I didn't know they came in colors. Give 'em to me assorted."

So the druggist fixed him up.

Ten months later Danny went to the drugstore and said, "Give me a maternity brassiere."

"What bust?" asked the druggist.

"One of those damned blue ones!" said Danny.

* * *

Did you hear about the seven guys and a girl who went fishing?

She came home with a red snapper.

* * *

Trevor went to his first orgy on Saturday night and on Monday his office co-worker Chuck asked, "How was it?"

"It's true, it's true!" moaned Trevor.

"What's true?" asked Chuck.

"That your whole life flashes before your eyes," he replied, "when you're being gone down on for the third time!"

* * *

CONVERSATION PIECE

A girl men like to talk about

A taxi streaking through the Bronx late one night suddenly came to a screeching stop.

"What's the idea of stopping here?" asked the guy in the rear seat.

The cab driver said, "I thought I hoid the goil say 'Stop!' Didn't she?"

"Yes. But she wasn't talking to you. Now keep going."

Having terminated their relationship rather abruptly, he was naturally shamefaced at running into her again on the street.

"Tell me," he said, with a rather painful attempt at small talk, "how's that diet of yours progressing?"

"Just fine," she answered. "Last week I took off eight pounds."

"That's wonderful. How did you ever do it?"

"I had your baby!"

* * *

Walter: I go out only with girls who wear glasses.
Cynthia: Why?
Walter: So I can breathe on them and they can't see what I'm doing.

* * *

A gal whose particular vice
Was to make herself dongs of ice
    Explained, "While they're chilly
    And perhaps somewhat silly
They cool my device very nice!"

* * *

Rosalind and Frank finished their love-making. Rosalind began urinating over the edge of a cliff into a lake. "Look," she said, "I peed right into that canoe down there."

"That's no canoe. That's your reflection."

Claude went to a swinging singles bar and soon began chatting with a sexy redhead. Suddenly he noticed a hair protruding from between her voluptuous boobs.

It looked so enticing, Claude reached out and pulled the hair. Instantly the girl's hands dropped to her crotch as she shouted: "Ouch!"

* * *

"Boy, was I drunk!" announced Derrick to his friend. "We had a little drink and I kissed her on the lips. Then we had another little drink and both got undressed."

"Then what happened?"

"We had another drink and I kissed her on the nipples."

"Yes?"

"And another little drink and I kissed her on the belly-button."

"Yes? Yes?"

"Oh, boy was I drunk!"

* * *

Ambitious Aylwin was bored with his fellow mailroom worker, "You're dull, Daniel," he said.

"Why do you say that?"

"Perk up your vocabulary. When someone asks, 'How do you feel?' don't just say, 'Fine.' Instead, say, 'like a guy with a panty fetish who just landed a laundry job at the YWCA.' "

* * *

Ever since men began courting women to win their favors they developed unique approaches to accomplish the goal. Here are a few standard samples you may recognize:

"There's gonna be a major war within the next two years and I probably only have two years to live. Would you deny me pleasure in my short life?"

"How do you know you're not frigid?"

"Sex improves athletic ability. Don't you want us to win the big game Saturday?"

"Sex clears up pimples. Do you want me to be a scar face?"

"Look, I've been tested, I'm completely sterile. There's no way in the world . . ."

"I have this problem. I'm a borderline homosexual. You'd be doing me a favor. If you don't go to bed with me, I'll turn queer. You just can't let that happen. Please help me."

* * *

"How come you stopped dating Doris?" asked a friend.
"Aw, she keeps using four letter words!"
"Really? Which ones?"
"Don't! Can't! Won't!"

* * *

There was a young lady from Sidney
Who liked it right up to her kidney.
A man from Quebec
Shoved it up to her neck.
He had a big one—didn't he?

* . * . *

Darrell was undressing in the bedroom of his fifth floor east side apartment. Suddenly he noticed a pretty airline hostess doing the same thing across the airshaft in the next building. He became quickly aroused.

Darrell opened the window, laid his erection across from his windowsill to hers and said, "Come on over!"

"But," she hesitated, "how will I get back?"

* * *

The boss finally agreed to give Ken the afternoon off because he said his girlfriend was going to have a baby.

Next morning, the boss said, "Was it a boy or girl?"

"Too soon to tell," replied Ken. "We won't know for another nine months."

* * *

DESSERT DITTY

She was only the piemaker's daughter,
but she had lots of topping.

Ted took time off from his successful Philadelphia ad agency and now was living it up in the Bahamas. One afternoon on the beach he met Lynda, a pretty school teacher from Virginia. When Lynda admitted she couldn't swim, Ted led her into the water to help.

Two hours later, Lynda asked, "Look, will I really drown if you take your finger out?"

"How was your date last night?" asked Jules.

"Awful," replied Les, "beautiful but awful. The minute we got to her apartment, the phone started ringing—every guy in town wanted a date with her. We didn't have a moment's peace. I was fed up!"

"Hey," said Jules. "don't you expect a beautiful girl to have her number in the phone book?"

"Yes," growled Les, "but not in the Yellow Pages."

* * *

How can you tell a guy is getting older?

When he keeps asking at a group sex party: "What . . . my turn *again*?"

* * *

A pretty young maiden of France
Decided she'd just "take a chance."
    She let herself go
    For an hour or so,
And now all her sisters are aunts.

* * *

Sanford Schmidt, the popular Los Angeles Lothario, loves this little lulu:

Joanna brought Wilbur into the living room of her parents' home. "Honey," he said "we're going to have a wonderful time tonight, I have three tickets to the theater."

"But why do we need three tickets?" asked Joanna.

"Simple," he replied, "They're for your mother, father, and brother."

Highly sexed Dennis went to a doctor. "When in the company of the opposite sex," he explained, "I get an erection at the slightest provocation."

"Why don't you simply tape the organ to your leg," advised the M.D.

Three days later, the doctor ran into Dennis and asked him, "Did my advice work okay?"

"Everything went great till the end of my first date. She started up the steps of her house, and then she suddenly turned around and leaned down to kiss me—that's when I kicked her right in the face."

* * *

LOLA'S LYRIC

Here's to the night I met you.
If I hadn't met you, I wouldn't have
let you.
Now that I've let you, I'm glad I met you.
And I'll let you again, I'll bet you.

* * *

When a girl is invited to a man's apartment to see his etchings, it's usually not a standing invitation.

* * *

Glenn dutifully picked up his date Felicia at her house and as they were leaving the girl's mother said, "Young man, I want to see that Felicia gets home early tonight."

"Don't worry," said Glenn. "I'll have her in bed by ten o'clock."

Miranda lay on the bed naked yet she refused Bob's advances. "I'm on strike," she announced.

"Me too," said her boyfriend, "but I have a feeling I'm going to get a raise, then we'll both go to work."

* * *

There was a young lady from Balister,
Who was nicer by far than her sister:
    The sister would giggle
    And wiggle and jiggle,
But this one would come if you kissed her!

* * *

Harriet, a buxom blonde, went to a Philadelphia police station and walked up to the desk sergeant. She proceeded to give a detailed description of a man who had dragged her by the hair down three flights of stairs, threatened to choke her to death and finally beat her up.

"Don't worry," said the sergeant, "with that description, we'll have him arrested and put in jail in practically no time."

"But I don't want him arrested," said Harriet. "Just find him. He promised to marry me."

* * *

AN ORGY

Grope Therapy

Girl: (to the boy who is petting her) Oh, I feel so silly.

Boy: Well, reach in here and you'll feel nuts.

LOVER'S LOGIC

Maidens are like melons;
Shall I tell you why?
To plug a single good one,
You must a hundred try.

* * *

Augustina, an attractive but militant feminist, had been propositioned by a male stranger at a cocktail party. "I think you should know," she replied, "that I've developed an immunity to being used by men as a casual sex object."

"That's not surprising," answered the guy, "considering the number of times you've been inoculated."

* * *

Danny was deeply in love with Mae and wanted to propose but was too embarassed because of his tiny organ. The guy was so ashamed he wouldn't discuss it with her or even let her see him naked. Hoping to bring up the matter with the least embarrassment, he drove up into the hills with Mae one night.

Danny parked the car in a very black spot. Then he quietly unzipped and put his penis in the girl's hand.

"No, thanks," she said, "I don't smoke."

* * *

Call Girl Giggles

Alarice, a buxom blonde, was arrested for prostitution and brought to trial. "Have you anything to offer the gentlemen of the jury on your own behalf?"

"Oh, no, your Honor," she answered, "I've learned my lesson."

* * *

Anita and Ellamae, two ladies of the evening, met on Fifth Avenue. "You don't look too good, honey," said Anita.

"I've been sick for months, haven't eaten regularly, and I'm flat broke," said Ellamae. "Can you lend me $50 until I can get back on my back again?"

"It's time," wept a prostie of Loring,
"New avenues I was exploring,
    This street corner jazz
    Is a pain in the azz,
And the men you meet whoring are boring."

*   *   *

Claretta, a Baltimore call girl, had just finished with her John and he handed her three hundred-dollar bills. The girl was flabbergasted, for she'd never been given more than $50 before.

"It's nothing," said the man. "You come back tomorrow night and there'll be another $300 for you."

The following evening Claretta returned, and after they made love, he handed her $300. She thanked him and he said, "Don't mention it. Come back tomorrow night and there'll be another $300 for you."

Claretta returned and after she satisfied him he gave her another $300.

"You're the most generous man I've ever met," she said. "Where are you from?"

"Raleigh,"

"What a coincidence," she exclaimed. "My mother lives in Raleigh."

"I know," said the man. "When she heard I was coming to Baltimore, she gave me $900 to give to you."

154

How do you make a hormone?
Don't pay her.

* * *

Two well-dressed, matronly women entered the business office and approached an executive.

"Sir," said one, "we are soliciting funds for the welfare and rehabilitation of wayward women. Would you care to donate?"

"Sorry," replied the exec, "but I contribute directly."

* * *

Did you hear about the poor old prostie who lived in the desert so long that she ended up as a dry hump?

* * *

A crazy-looking character ran up to Crystal the streetwalker and whispered, "I don't have time to rent a room. Slip me a quickie before the trouble starts."

Crystal led him into an alley and took care of his needs. As they straightened out their clothing, she asked, "When is the trouble you mentioned going to begin?"

"Right now," he answered, "I don't have any money!"

* * *

Arabella went to her doctor with the complaint that she was a bleeder. "Doctor if I get the slightest cut on my finger, it bleeds for hours."

"That's interesting," said the M.D. "and what happens when you have your period? Then how much do you lose?"

Arabella replied, "About $500."

* * *

PIMP

A public relations man for a pubic relations girl

* * *

Marty Brill, the brilliant young comedian, cracks up audiences with this cajoler:

The call girl arrived at Talbot's hotel room and in 30 seconds she was flat on her back in bed, completely nude.

"I've heard of passionate men," she exclaimed, "but you take the cake. What's the big hurry?"

"Well," said Talbot, "I forgot that I sent for you and I just took a sleeping pill."

Did you hear about the new mouthwash for astrology-oriented call girls?

It's called: WHORE-O-SCOPE

Dominic's sister was the most popular girl in Brooklyn. She had more boyfriends than she knew what to do with, and she never wanted for a thing. Dominic was a poor musician, always in debt and constantly asking his sister for spending money.

One afternoon he tried to borrow $20 and she said, "What's wrong with you? I don't have any trouble saving money, so why should you?"

"Sure," he said, "but you've got money coming in all the time from the very thing that's keeping me broke."

* * *

A hush fell over the courtroom as the judge began speaking to the dainty defendant:

"This jury of thy peers hath recommended that I cause thee to wear a scarlet 'A' upon thy bosom for all to see. And let it be recorded that I deem this a most questionable recommendation. The jury hath not done thee true justice, Mistress Prynne."

"But, your Honor," interjected the jury foreman, " 'A' was the highest mark we could give her!"

* * *

In a small northwestern town, the preacher wanted to build a new church. One day the clergyman called the leading townsmen to discuss fund raising. In the middle of the meeting the bawdy house madam entered the room and said:

"Preacher, here's $10,000 to help build your center."

"Oh, no!" said the man of God. "We can't take your money. It's tainted."

"But," insisted the madam, "you're having trouble raising the money. As a matter of fact, I'll make it $20,000."

"Go away," answered the clergyman. "Your money is not clean—we don't want your money."

One of the citizens shouted, "go ahead take it, Reverend. It's not her money—it's ours!"

* * *

HORIZON

Call girl getting out of the sack

* * *

I fell in love with a girl named Charlotte
    Despite the fact that she was a harlot
Perhaps, intrigued by her fair name,
    I forgot her home was of ill fame.
Yes, I can look at life with glee
    What hundreds paid for, I got free!

* * *

One freezing cold night a Broadway pimp was getting into bed with his woman when a John knocked on the door. The pimp quickly climbed out on the fire escape in his underwear. As he shivered with cold, the client inside enjoyed himself in the bed the pimp had warmed.

The customer spent the next two hours drinking, making love, and eating in bed. Finally, he lit up one of the pimp's cigars and left.

The whore rushed to the window, and helped in the half-frozen pimp.

"Well," asked the pimp, blue with cold, "has the sucker gone yet?"

* * *

What's brown and fuzzy and lays in the forest?

Smokey the prostitute.

* * *

Did you hear about the two call girls who went on the Too-Late Show and blew the whole network?

* * *

A very expensive lady of the evening, Louise, met Rudy at a bar and after a few drinks he invited her up to his apartment to see his orchids.

When they got to Rudy's apartment, the room was full of orchids. "Well, I'll be darned," exclaimed Louise.

"Do you like orchids?" he asked.

"I suppose so," she replied, wondering when he'd get down to business.

"If you do," said Rudy, "let's go in the bedroom, I've got some beauties in there."

"This is it," thought Louise. She eagerly entered, and of all things, more orchids. She explored, "Listen, you jerk, I didn't come up here just to look at orchids."

Which just goes to prove that you can't lead a horticulture.

* * *

HORTICULTURIST

*An etiquette consultant
in a house of ill repute*

* * *

Porterfield spotted a pretty blonde at an uptown Manhattan cocktail party. He took an immediate liking to her and whispered, "Would you consider spending the night with me for a million dollars?"

"Yes," answered the girl immediately.

"Would you do it for twenty dollars?"

"Say," snapped the blonde, "what do you think I am!"

"We've established that," replied Porterfield, "now we're trying to agree on the price!"

* * *

Did you hear what happened to the hooker who didn't know the difference between putty and vaseline?

All her windows fell out!

*   *   *

A bordello outside Philadelphia was well known for offering ladies from every corner of the globe. Since the girls ate a variety of foods, the Madame employed several chefs who specialized in the cuisine of each nation represented. The girls loved the gourmet delights and slowly began to lose their voluptuous figures. Soon they got so fat they lost all of their customers.

MORAL: Too many cooks spoil the brothel!

HERE LIES SALLY
JO LEETERS

WHO, INSIDE HER-
SELF BURIED MANY
A BONE

·

BUT NO MORE WILL
SHE PLAY WITH
PETERS

·

AT LAST SHE
SLEEPS ALONE

163

Gilmore was about to check into a hotel in Dallas when he noticed a ravishing redhead smiling at him.

Gilmore walked over to her and they chatted for a few moments. Soon he returned to the desk with her clinging to his arm and they registered as man and wife.

Two days later Gilmore checked out and was handed a bill for $2,500. "There's some mistake here," he protested, "I've only been here two days."

"Yes," explained the clerk, "but your wife has been here for two months."

* * *

Dobbs, an offshore oil driller, came to town for the first time in weeks, went to the bawdy house and asked for the roughest, toughest girl in the house.

"Nobody tougher than Bonnie," said the madame. "Go on up to room 12 and I'll send her along."

"Okay," said Dobbs, "and tell her to bring a couple of beers."

Ten minutes later Bonnie arrived, put two bottles of beer on the dresser, pulled off her flimsy gown and then positioned herself on the floor on her knees and elbows.

"No, no!" exclaimed the oil worker. "In the bed, and in the old-fashioned way."

"Sure," beamed Bonnie, "but I thought you might wanna open them beers first."

SIGN OVER BIDET IN BAWDY HOUSE

*The love bug will bite you if
you don't wash out!*

* * *

Murray went to a red-light house and told the madame, "I need something real unusual to satisfy me."

"Okay," said the lady of the house. "Go into room 220!"

Inside the room, Murray found a chicken. He chased it all over the place and finally 20 minutes later, totally exhausted he captured the fowl.

A week later, Murray returned and again asked for something different. This time the madame sent him to room 221!

There were several people waiting there. In a few minutes one of the walls slid opened and exposed three women and two men who were wrapped up in each other in an orgy.

Murray turned to the man next to him and said, "Hey, this is pretty good!"

"It's nothing!" said the man. "You should've been here last week. Some guy was running around the room trying to screw a chicken!"

* * *

Did you hear the one about the hooker who had two twats?

The other girls didn't like her, though. She walked around with that "holier than thou" attitude.

Birnbaum went to a brothel and announced to the madam, "I want you to know in advance, I'm a terrible person. A monster, a pervert. I like to beat women and I got my own whip specially made for me. You got anybody for a terrible person like me?"

"Oh, sure," said the flesh peddler, "Hildegarde'll do it. But beating comes pretty high. It'll cost you five hundred bucks."

"Well, what am I gonna do? I'm depraved and I gotta gratify my desires, no matter what it costs."

Birnbaum took Hildegarde upstairs. She insisted on the money up front so he gave her the five hundred. Birnbaum then pulled out a leather whip and began beating the girl with it mercilessly.

After awhile she gasped, "I can't . . . take much more! W-W-When . . . are you going . . . to quit?"

"When . . . you give me . . . back my five hundred!"

A Union organizer went to a bawdy house and looked over the girls. "I'll take that one," he said pointing to a cute little blonde.

"Oh, no, you're a Union man, you'll take that one," said the madam, pointing to an old hag sitting in the corner. "She's got seniority rights."

* * *

There's a new cereal on the market called Hooker. It doesn't snap, crackle or pop. It just lays there and bangs.

* * *

Shapiro hired a hooker and throughout their lovemaking he kept exclaiming, "Phooey! Phooey!"

The girl was a little hurt over his remark and when they finished she asked, "Why did you keep saying 'Phooey'? Wasn't I good enough for you?"

"Don't misunderstand," said Shapiro. "*You* were fine. When I said 'Phooey' I was thinking of my wife."

* * *

SCREWBALL

A dance held in a bordello

* * *

MADAME

One who offers vice to the lovelorn

*   *   *

Did you hear about the pimp who has so many girls on the street that he's up to his alligators in ass?

*   *   *

A class of minority school kids were taken to a farm outside Los Angeles to give them experience in the rural life.

The farmer held up a tool and the teacher said, "José, can you tell me what that is?"

"A shovel," answered the Mexican child.

The farmer held up another tool. "What is that, Wing To?" asked the teacher.

"A rake," replied the Chinese boy.

Once again the farmer held up a tool. "What could that be, Willie?" asked the teacher.

"I dunno," said the black boy.

"That's a hoe," explained the teacher.

"No ma'am. That ain't no hoe. My sister's a hoe, and she don't look like that!"

*   *   *